HAMLYN
ALL COLOUR
HEALTHY

LOW FAT　　　LOW GI　　　LOW CARB

HAMLYN
ALL COLOUR
HEALTHY

hamlyn

- Both metric and imperial measurements are given for the recipes. Use one set of measures only, not a mixture of both.

- Ovens should be preheated to the specified temperature. If using a fan-assisted oven, follow the manufacturer's instructions for adjusting the time and temperature. Grills should also be preheated.

- This book includes dishes made with nuts and nut derivatives. It is advisable for those with known allergic reactions to nuts and nut derivatives and those who may be potentially vulnerable to these allergies, such as pregnant and nursing mothers, invalids, the elderly, babies and children, to avoid dishes made with nuts and nut oils. It is also prudent to check the labels of preprepared ingredients for the possible inclusion of nut derivatives.

- The Department of Health advises that eggs should not be consumed raw. This book contains some dishes made with raw or lightly cooked eggs. It is prudent for more vulnerable people such as pregnant and nursing mothers, invalids, the elderly, babies and young children to avoid uncooked or lightly cooked dishes made with eggs.

- Meat and poultry should be cooked thoroughly. To test if poultry is cooked, pierce the flesh through the thickest part with a skewer or fork – the juices should run clear, never pink or red.

- Where pepper is listed in the recipe ingredients, always use freshly ground black pepper.

- All the recipes in this book have been analysed by a professional nutritionist. The analysis refers to each serving.

First published in Great Britain in 2006 by Hamlyn,
a division of Octopus Publishing Group Ltd
2–4 Heron Quays, London E14 4JP

Copyright © Octopus Publishing Group Ltd 2006

ISBN-13: 9780600613626

ISBN-10: 0 600 61362 3

A CIP catalogue record for this book is available from the British Library

Printed and bound in China

10 9 8 7 6 5 4 3 2 1

Contents

Introduction

Healthy living

A healthy lifestyle is a combination of factors, but the best place to start is with your diet. If you eat well, you'll improve your general wellbeing, as a healthy, well-balanced diet will provide your body with all its nutritional needs. Regular exercise, good sleep patterns and trying to avoid stress are other important elements that will complete the picture, but a healthy diet will have a positive impact on your whole life and it's something you can have total control over. There are many small, immediate changes you can make to your eating habits that will have a positive impact on your health. Here are just a few:

Eat regularly

By eating at regular times, you should avoid the slumps that lead to hunger pangs and snacking. If you feel hungry between meals, have a piece of fruit, some raisins or nuts.

Don't skip breakfast

Your mum was right – this is the most important meal of the day! Breakfast kick starts your metabolism and will stop you eating too much during the rest of the day.

Late-night munchies

If you eat just before going to bed, your body doesn't have time to digest the food properly and this can cause stomach cramps and insomnia, especially if you have a large meal.

Change your oil

Olive oil contains beneficial fats, so use this for cooking and dressing salads instead of vegetable or sunflower oil.

Reduce your sugar and salt intakes

Salt and sugar are often added to processed foods, including breakfast cereals, bread and canned goods, so when you're cooking, try to avoid adding salt to your food and don't put any on the table.

Get grilling

Switch to low-fat cooking techniques such as grilling and baking.

Say cheese

If you eat a lot of dairy products, change to lower-fat varieties.

Recipe for success

Healthy eating doesn't mean that you have to miss out on interesting meals, eat tiny portions or constantly watch what you eat. Once you have adjusted to a more balanced diet that's rich in fresh fruit and vegetables, fish, lean meat and pulses, and is lower in fat, salt and sugar, you'll find that the options for delicious meals are endless. This new recipe collection contains ideas for every meal and occasion, from breakfasts to three-course dinners, so entertaining needn't be off the menu either. All the recipes in the book have been analysed for their nutritional content, and recipes that are low in fat or carbohydrates, or that have a low Glycaemic Index, have been highlighted to make it easier for you to plan your daily meals.

Fat

As a guideline, women are advised to consume no more than 70 g (2½ oz) of fat per day and men no more than 95 g (3⅓ oz). Contrary to popular belief, certain fats are actually beneficial to us and should be eaten in moderation as part of a balanced diet. Fat provides our bodies with energy, but the problem arises when we consume more fat than can be burnt off and is subsequently stored as surplus. In general, good fats are those that naturally occur in foods and haven't been processed or refined. So, for example, the fats in nuts, oily fish and olive oil (monounsaturated and polyunsaturated fats) are good, whereas the fats found in processed foods such as meat products, biscuits, crisps and full-fat dairy products (unsaturated fats) are bad and should be avoided or limited in the diet.

Carbohydrates

Carbohydrates consist of sugars and starches. They provide the fuel that our bodies need to keep us going and are therefore an essential part of our daily food requirements. However, as with fats, there are different types of carbohydrate – simple and complex – and it's important that we eat the right kind. Simple carbohydrates are basically sugars and they don't provide much in terms of nutritional benefits for our bodies. They are found in processed foods, such as ready-meals, and other products that contain refined sugars, such as carbonated drinks, sweets, cakes and biscuits. Instead, we should be concentrating on the complex, or beneficial, carbohydrates, and these tend to be found in foods that are unrefined. Examples are leafy green vegetables, beans, grains and rice. From a health perspective, the less refined a carbohydrate is, the better it is.

The Glycaemic Index

The Glycaemic Index, or GI, is a number that is allocated to a specific food depending on the effect it has on your blood glucose level. It is linked to the carbohydrate content of a food and works on the principle that a food based on simple carbohydrates will break down quickly, giving a sudden glucose peak, whereas complex carbs break down more slowly, evening out glucose levels and helping to eliminate sudden hunger pangs and cravings. Other factors are taken into account, such as the protein and fat content, as these can also have an impact on the breakdown of carbohydrates.

Food for life

The most important thing to remember is that you should enjoy your food. Eating is one of life's pleasures and it's fine to treat yourself every so often, as long as you stick to good, wholesome, healthy food the rest of the time. The recipes in this book have been chosen for their health-giving properties, but also for their diversity, the wonderful ingredients they use and the enjoyment you will get from preparing and eating them.

Stocks

Most of the recipes in this book are self-contained and can be made without reference to other sections of the book, but many of the soups, and some of the meat dishes, use stock. Although you can, of course, make up the required quantity of stock from cubes or powder, home-made stock will give a recipe extra depth of flavour – and you can be sure that there is no extra salt or colouring. Making your own stock is well worth the time and small amount of effort involved. If you do not already have your own favourite stock recipe, use one of the following as directed in the recipe.

Beef stock

Preparation time:
10 minutes

Cooking time:
about 4¼ hours

Makes:
about 1.5 litres (2½ pints)

750 g (1½ lb) shin of beef, cubed
2 onions, chopped
2–3 carrots, chopped
1 bay leaf
1 bouquet garni
4–6 peppercorns
1.8 litres (3 pints) water
½ teaspoon salt

Put all the ingredients into a large saucepan. Bring slowly to the boil, then immediately reduce the heat to a slow simmer. Cover the pan with a well-fitting lid and simmer for 4 hours, removing any scum that rises to the surface. Strain the stock through a muslin-lined sieve and leave to cool before refrigerating.

Fish stock

Preparation time:
10 minutes

Cooking time:
about 30 minutes

Makes:
about 1.8 litres (3 pints)

1.5 kg (3 lb) fish trimmings, from any fish excluding oily fish
1 onion, sliced
1 small leek, white part only, sliced
1 celery stick, chopped
1 bay leaf
6 parsley stalks
10 peppercorns
475 ml (16 fl oz) dry white wine
1.8 litres (3 pints) water

Put all the ingredients into a large saucepan. Bring slowly to just below boiling point and simmer very gently for 20 minutes, removing any scum that rises to the surface. Strain the stock through a muslin-lined sieve and leave to cool before refrigerating.

Chicken stock

Preparation time:
10 minutes

Cooking time:
about 2¼–2¾ hours

Makes:
about 1 litre (1¾ pints)

1 cooked chicken carcass
raw giblets and trimmings (optional)
1 onion, chopped
2–3 carrots, chopped
1 celery stick, chopped
1 bay leaf
3–4 parsley stalks
1 thyme sprig
1.8 litres (3 pints) water

Chop the chicken carcass into 3 or 4 pieces and put them into a large saucepan with the remaining ingredients. Bring slowly to the boil, removing any scum that rises to the surface. Reduce the heat and simmer for 2–2½ hours. Strain the stock through a muslin-lined sieve and leave to cool before refrigerating.

Vegetable stock

Preparation time:
10 minutes

Cooking time:
about 40 minutes

Makes:
1 litre (1¾ pints)

500 g (1 lb) mixed vegetables (excluding potatoes, parsnips and other starchy root vegetables), chopped
1 garlic clove
6 peppercorns
1 bouquet garni
1.2 litres (2 pints) water

Put all the ingredients into a large saucepan. Bring slowly to the boil and simmer gently for 30 minutes, removing any scum that rises to the surface if necessary. Strain the stock through a muslin-lined sieve and leave to cool before refrigerating.

1 Breakfasts

1 Berry and rice muesli

2 Strawberry muesli

Preparation time:
5–10 minutes

Serves: **4**

125 g (4 oz) brown rice, cooked
50 g (2 oz) millet flakes
25 g (1 oz) sunflower seeds
50 g (2 oz) seedless raisins or sultanas
125 g (4 oz) ready-to-eat dried
strawberries or cranberries
25 g (1 oz) desiccated coconut or fresh
grated coconut

TO SERVE:
semi-skimmed milk or low-fat natural
yogurt
fresh apple

Combine all the ingredients. Divide the muesli between 4 bowls and serve with milk or yogurt and fresh apple.

This muesli will keep well in an airtight container for up to 3 weeks.

Preparation time:
10 minutes

Cooking time:
2–2½ hours

Oven temperature:
110°C (225°F) Gas Mark ¼

Makes: **14 servings**

250 g (8 oz) strawberries, thinly sliced
250 g (8 oz) rolled oats
75 g (3 oz) flaked almonds
75 g (3 oz) pumpkin seeds
75 g (3 oz) sunflower seeds
25 g (1 oz) golden linseeds
75 g (3 oz) ready-to-eat dried cranberries,
roughly chopped
semi-skimmed milk, to serve

Blot away any juice from the strawberries with kitchen paper and arrange them in a single layer on a baking sheet lined with greaseproof paper. Bake in a preheated oven, 110°C (225°F), Gas Mark ¼, for 1 hour, then turn them over and continue to cook for a further 1–1½ hours, or until crisp. Allow to cool.

Mix together all the remaining ingredients, then carefully stir in the strawberries and transfer the muesli to an airtight container. To serve, pour the muesli into bowls and add a splash of milk. This muesli will keep well in an airtight container for up to 3 weeks.

NUTRITIONAL INFORMATION Shop-bought muesli can be loaded with sugar, salt and fat. This version relies only on fruit sugars for sweetness and its low-GI value will help you feel full for longer.

303 kcals (1271 kj) ■ low fat ■ low GI ■ high fibre ■
source of phytoestrogens

NUTRITIONAL INFORMATION Seeds are rich in omega-3 and omega-6 fatty acids. These are essential for heart health, immunity, the nervous system and the brain.

189 kcals (792 kj) ■ low fat ■ low GI ■ high fibre ■
source of omega-3 and -6 fatty acids

3 Pumpkin seed and apricot muesli

4 Mixed-grain porridge

Preparation time:
10 minutes

Serves: 2

50 g (2 oz) rolled jumbo oats
1 tablespoon seedless sultanas or raisins
1 tablespoon pumpkin or sunflower seeds
1 tablespoon chopped almonds
25 g (1 oz) ready-to-eat dried apricots, chopped
2 tablespoons fruit juice, such as apple or orange juice, or water
2 small dessert apples, peeled and grated
3 tablespoons semi-skimmed milk or low-fat natural yogurt

Divide the oats, sultanas or raisins, seeds, almonds and apricots between 2 bowls and pour in the fruit juice or water. Add the grated apple and stir it in, then top the muesli with milk or yogurt.

For a softer texture, soak the oats and sultanas or raisins with the fruit juice or water overnight.

Preparation time:
5 minutes

Cooking time:
13–15 minutes

Serves: 3

450 ml (¾ pint) semi-skimmed milk
25 g (1 oz) millet grains
25 g (1 oz) barley flakes
25 g (1 oz) rolled oats

TO SERVE:
fromage frais
muscovado sugar
ready-to-eat dried fruit, such as apricots and cranberries, chopped

Pour the milk into a saucepan and bring to the boil, then add the millet grains, barley flakes and oats. Reduce the heat and simmer for 8–10 minutes, stirring occasionally, until the mixture is thick and soft.

Spoon the porridge into bowls. Top with fromage frais and sprinkle with a little muscovado sugar and chopped ready-to-eat dried fruit.

NUTRITIONAL INFORMATION Oats are a good source of soluble fibre, which helps lower blood cholesterol.

337 kcals (1415 kj) ■ **low GI** ■ **high fibre** ■ **source of phytoestrogens** ■ **source of vitamins C and E**

147 kcals (619 kj) ■ **low fat** ■ **low GI** ■ **high fibre** ■ **source of potassium**

5 Banana muffins with cinnamon topping

6 Prune and vanilla muffins

Preparation time:
15 minutes

Cooking time:
25–30 minutes

Oven temperature:
200°C (400°F) Gas Mark 6

Makes: **6**

100 g (3½ oz) plain wholemeal flour
25 g (1 oz) soya flour
3 tablespoons light muscovado sugar
2 teaspoons baking powder
1 egg, beaten
50 ml (2 fl oz) soya milk
50 ml (2 fl oz) sunflower oil
2 ripe bananas, about 200 g (7 oz) when peeled, roughly mashed

TOPPING:
1 tablespoon golden linseeds
25 g (1 oz) self-raising flour, sifted
15 g (½ oz) butter, at room temperature
40 g (1½ oz) demerara sugar
½ teaspoon ground cinnamon
1 tablespoon water

Line a deep 6-section muffin tin with paper muffin cases. To make the topping, put the linseeds into a food processor and whiz for 30 seconds. Put the self-raising flour into a bowl and rub in the butter with the fingertips until the mixture resembles fine breadcrumbs. Add the demerara sugar, linseeds and cinnamon, then stir in the measurement water and mix well.

Mix together the flours, sugar and baking powder in a bowl and make a well in the centre. In a separate bowl, mix together the egg, milk and oil. Pour the liquid ingredients into the dry ones and stir until just combined. Stir in the bananas, taking care not to over-mix.

Fill the muffin cases two-thirds full with the mixture, then sprinkle a little of the topping over each muffin. Bake in a preheated oven, 200°C (400°F), Gas Mark 6, for 25–30 minutes, or until a skewer inserted into the centre comes out clean. Transfer the muffins to a wire rack to cool.

250 kcals (1047 kj) ■ **low fat** ■ **source of phytoestrogens** ■ **source of potassium**

Preparation time:
15 minutes

Cooking time:
18–20 minutes

Oven temperature:
190°C (375°F) Gas Mark 5

Makes: **12**

50 g (2 oz) sugar lumps (optional)
300 g (10 oz) plain flour
3 teaspoons baking powder
125 g (4 oz) light muscovado sugar
175 g (6 oz) stoned prunes, roughly chopped
3 eggs
4 tablespoons sunflower oil
50 g (2 oz) butter, melted
1½ teaspoons vanilla extract
150 g (5 oz) low-fat natural yogurt

Line a deep 12-section muffin tin with paper muffin cases. Put the sugar lumps into a polythene bag, if using, and roughly crush with a rolling pin.

Put the flour, baking powder and sugar into a large bowl, add the prunes and stir to mix. Beat together the eggs, oil, melted butter and vanilla extract in a small bowl and add to the flour mixture. Add the yogurt and stir gently until just combined.

Divide the mixture between the muffin cases, sprinkle with the crushed sugar, if using, and bake in a preheated oven, 190°C (375°F), Gas Mark 5, for 18–20 minutes, or until the muffins are well risen and the tops have cracked. Serve while still warm.

COOK'S NOTES The secret of successful muffin-making is almost to under-mix them; don't worry too much if there are tiny patches of flour – over-mixing muffins makes them heavy.

266 kcals (1115 kj) ■ **low fat** ■ **high fibre** ■ **source of iron** ■ **source of vitamin A**

7 Pain perdu with fruit compôte

8 Light 'n' low pancakes

Preparation time.
10 minutes, plus cooling

Cooking time:
about 15 minutes

Serves: 2

2 slices of mixed-seed bread
1 egg, beaten
3 tablespoons semi-skimmed milk
1 drop of vanilla extract or a pinch of
   ground cinnamon
15 g (½ oz) butter
2 tablespoons golden caster sugar

SUMMER FRUIT COMPOTE:
250 g (8 oz) mixed summer fruit, such
   as raspberries, blueberries and
   strawberries, defrosted if frozen
finely grated rind and juice of 1 large
   orange
1 tablespoon redcurrant jelly

Preparation time:
10 minutes, plus standing

Cooking time:
about 30 minutes

Oven temperature:
190°C (375°F) Gas Mark 5

Serves: 4

125 g (4 oz) plain wholemeal flour
1 egg
325 ml (11 fl oz) semi-skimmed milk
1 teaspoon vegetable oil, plus a little
   extra for cooking

TOPPING IDEAS:
mixed berries
chopped fresh fruit
chopped apple, raisins and
   ground cinnamon
cottage cheese
low-fat cream cheese
fruit spread or preserve

First, to make the fruit compote, put the fruit, orange rind and juice and redcurrant jelly into a large saucepan. Cover the pan and cook gently for 5 minutes, or until the juices flow and the fruit is soft. Remove the pan from the heat and allow to cool.

Cut the slices of bread in half diagonally. Beat together the egg, milk and vanilla extract or cinnamon in a shallow dish. Dip the bread slices in the egg mixture until well coated.

Heat the butter in a frying pan until foaming, add the bread and sprinkle over half the sugar. Fry over a medium heat for 2–3 minutes. Turn the bread slices over, sprinkle with the remaining sugar and cook for a further 2 minutes.

Serve the pain perdu immediately with the fruit compôte.

Sift the flour into a bowl, adding the bran in the sieve to the flour.

In a separate bowl, beat together the egg, milk and oil, then slowly add to the flour. Stir until a smooth batter forms. Leave the batter to stand for about 20 minutes, then stir again.

Heat a little oil in a nonstick frying pan. When the oil is hot, add 2 tablespoons of the pancake mixture and shake the pan so that it spreads. Cook the pancake for 2 minutes until the underside is lightly browned, then flip or turn it over and cook the other side for 1–2 minutes. Keep the pancake warm in a preheated oven, 190°C (375°F), Gas Mark 5, while you cook the remainder – you can stack one on top of the other as they are cooked. The mixture should make 8 pancakes. Serve with your chosen topping.

350 kcals (1468 kj) ■ **low fat** ■ **low GI** ■ **high fibre** ■
source of phytoestrogens

141 kcals (591 kj) ■ **low fat** ■ **high fibre**

9 Cinnamon tofu toast with poached plums

10 Mixed rice kedgeree with kippers

Preparation time:	400 g (13 oz) red plums, halved and
10 minutes	stoned
	50 g (2 oz) golden caster sugar, plus
Cooking time:	4 teaspoons
10 minutes	100 ml (3½ fl oz) water
	2 thick slices of sweet bread, such as
Serves: **2**	brioche or panettone
	125 g (4 oz) firm tofu, drained
	¼ teaspoon ground cinnamon

Put the plums into a heavy-based saucepan with the 50 g (2 oz) sugar and the measurement water. Heat gently, stirring, until the sugar has dissolved. Cover and simmer gently for 5 minutes, or until the plums have softened but are not falling apart.

Lightly toast the bread on one side. Pat the tofu dry on kitchen paper and cut it into very thin slices. Arrange the slices on the untoasted sides of the bread. Mix together the remaining 4 teaspoons sugar with the cinnamon and sprinkle over the tofu. Cook under a preheated moderate grill until the bread is toasted and the tofu is beginning to colour.

Spoon the poached plums and some of the cooking syrup into shallow serving bowls. Serve the toasts with the plums.

299 kcals (1250 kj) ■ **low fat** ■ **source of protein** ■ **source of vitamins B and C**

Preparation time:	75 g (3 oz) wild rice
15 minutes	175 g (6 oz) basmati rice
	325 g (11 oz) kipper fillets
Cooking time:	25 g (1 oz) butter
50–55 minutes	1 small onion, chopped
	1 small garlic clove, chopped
Serves: **4**	grated rind and juice of 1 lemon
	1 tablespoon curry paste
	1 teaspoon turmeric
	4 ripe tomatoes, skinned, deseeded and
	diced
	50 g (2 oz) seedless sultanas
	2 tablespoons chopped coriander leaves
	2 tablespoons chopped parsley
	salt and pepper
	1 hard-boiled egg, shelled and quartered,
	to garnish

Cook the wild rice in a saucepan of lightly salted boiling water for 45–50 minutes, or according to the packet instructions. Cook the basmati rice in a large saucepan of lightly salted boiling water for 15 minutes.

Meanwhile, steep the kippers in boiling water for 8–10 minutes until they are cooked. Drain well and pat dry with kitchen paper. Skin the fillets and discard any large bones, then carefully flake the flesh.

Melt the butter in a saucepan and fry the onion, garlic, lemon rind, curry paste and turmeric for 5 minutes. Add the tomatoes, sultanas and lemon juice and cook for a further 10 minutes. Drain the rice and add to the saucepan with the kippers, herbs and salt and pepper to taste. Stir over a low heat for 4–5 minutes until warmed through. Transfer the kedgeree to a warmed platter, garnish with the egg quarters and serve immediately.

453 kcals (1894 kj) ■ **low GI** ■ **source of omega-3 fatty acids** ■ **source of vitamins A and D**

11 Blueberry, peach and citrus salad

Preparation time:
10 minutes

Serves: **4**

200 g (7 oz) blueberries
2 oranges, segmented
2 grapefruits, segmented
2 ripe peaches, skinned, halved, stoned and sliced
50 g (2 oz) toasted wholegrains
300 g (10 oz) low-fat natural yogurt
2 teaspoons maple syrup

Divide the prepared fruit between 4 bowls. Mix together the toasted wholegrains, yogurt and maple syrup and spoon over the fruit. Serve.

 COOK'S NOTES If you can't find wholegrains in your local health-food shop or supermarket, replace them with toasted mixed nuts.

236 kcals (987 kj) ■ **low fat** ■ **low GI** ■ **source of antioxidants** ■ **source of vitamin C**

12 Watermelon and strawberry blush

Preparation time:
5 minutes

Serves: **2**

1 kg (2 lb) piece of watermelon
200 g (7 oz) strawberries, hulled
juice of 1 lime

Use a large spoon to scoop the melon flesh away from the skin and put it into a food processor or blender. Add the strawberries and whiz briefly until the fruits are just mixed.

Pour the fruit purée into a sieve set over a large jug, then press the pulp through the sieve until only the black seeds remain.

Mix the fruit purée with the lime juice, then pour into 2 glasses and serve immediately.

NUTRITIONAL INFORMATION Strawberries and limes are both packed with vitamin C, and watermelon contains such a high proportion of water that the finished drink does not need to be diluted. This delicious juice is pure fruit.

183 kcals (765 kj) ■ **low fat** ■ **source of antioxidants** ■ **source of vitamin C**

13 Banana and mango smoothie

14 Gingered apple and carrot juice

Preparation time:
5 minutes, plus freezing

Serves: **1**

1 small ripe banana, about 100 g (3½ oz)
250 ml (8 fl oz) semi-skimmed milk
1 small ripe mango, peeled, stoned and
   diced

Peel and slice the banana, then put the slices into a freezer container and freeze for at least 2 hours or overnight.

Put the chilled banana slices into a food processor or blender with the milk and mango and whiz until thick and frothy. Pour into a glass and serve immediately.

Preparation time:
10 minutes

Serves: **2**

375 g (12 oz) carrots, peeled and cut into
   chunks
3 apples, cored and cut into chunks
2.5 cm (1 inch) piece of fresh root ginger,
   peeled

Feed the carrot and apple chunks through a juicer with the ginger. Pour the juice into 2 tumblers and serve immediately.

NUTRITIONAL INFORMATION Mangoes are the best fruit source of the antioxidant vitamins A, C and E.

296 kcals (1237 kj) ■ low fat ■ low GI ■ high fibre ■ source of antioxidants ■ source of potassium

NUTRITIONAL INFORMATION This vibrant juice is packed with carotenoids. These are converted to vitamin A by the body. They are particularly important for normal tissue growth and are an antioxidant.

116 kcals (485 kj) ■ low fat ■ low GI ■ source of antioxidants ■ source of vitamins A and C

15 Walnut and banana sunrise smoothie

16 Fruity summer milk shake

Preparation time:
10 minutes

Serves: **2**

1 orange, segmented
1 banana, peeled and cut into chunks
150 ml (¼ pint) semi-skimmed milk
150 g (5 oz) low-fat natural yogurt
25 g (1 oz) chopped walnuts
3 teaspoons clear honey

Put all the ingredients into a food processor or blender and whiz until smooth and frothy. Pour into 2 glasses and serve immediately.

Preparation time:
5 minutes

Serves: **2**

1 ripe peach, skinned, halved, stoned and
chopped
150 g (5 oz) strawberries, hulled
150 g (5 oz) raspberries
200 ml (7 fl oz) semi-skimmed milk

Put the peach into a food processor or blender with the strawberries and raspberries and whiz to a purée, scraping the mixture down from the sides of the bowl if necessary.

Add the milk and blend the ingredients again until the mixture is smooth and frothy. To serve, pour the milk shake into 2 tall glasses.

NUTRITIONAL INFORMATION Nuts are high in fibre, rich in a wide range of vitamins and minerals and a good source of protein.

240 kcals (1003 kj) ▪ low fat ▪ low GI ▪ high fibre ▪ source of potassium ▪ source of protein

COOK'S NOTES You can use any mixture of soft summer fruits in this recipe, such as nectarines, redcurrants or blackberries. Depending how sweet the fruit is, you might need to add a little extra honey.

100 kcals (418 kj) ▪ low GI ▪ high fibre ▪ source of antioxidants ▪ source of vitamin C

2 Soups

17 Fennel and lemon soup

18 Fennel and butter bean soup

Preparation time:
20 minutes

Cooking time:
about 30 minutes

Serves: **4**

50 ml (2 fl oz) olive oil
3 large spring onions, chopped
250 g (8 oz) fennel bulb, trimmed, cored and finely sliced
1 potato, peeled and diced
finely grated rind and juice of 1 lemon
900 ml (1½ pints) Chicken or Vegetable Stock (see Introduction)
salt and pepper
toasted crusty bread, to serve (optional)

BLACK OLIVE GREMOLATA:
1 small garlic clove, finely chopped
finely grated rind of 1 lemon
4 tablespoons chopped parsley
16 black Greek olives, pitted and chopped

Heat the oil in a large saucepan and fry the spring onions for 5–10 minutes, or until soft. Add the fennel, potato and lemon rind and cook for 5 minutes until the fennel begins to soften. Pour in the stock and bring to the boil. Reduce the heat, cover the pan and simmer for about 15 minutes, or until the ingredients are tender.

Meanwhile, to make the gremolata, mix together the garlic, lemon rind and parsley, then stir in the olives. Cover and chill until required.

Whiz the soup in a food processor or blender and pass it through a sieve to remove any strings of fennel. The soup should not be too thick, so add more stock if necessary. Return the soup to the rinsed pan. Taste and season well with salt and pepper and lemon juice, then heat through gently. Pour the soup into warmed bowls and sprinkle with some gremolata, to be stirred in before eating. Serve with slices of toasted crusty bread, if liked.

163 kcals (684 kj) ■ low carb ■ low GI ■ source of vitamins C and E

Preparation time:
15 minutes

Cooking time:
35 minutes

Serves: **4**

900 ml (1½ pints) Vegetable Stock (see Introduction)
2 fennel bulbs, trimmed, cored and chopped
1 onion, chopped
1 courgette, chopped
1 carrot, chopped
2 garlic cloves, finely sliced
6 tomatoes, skinned and finely chopped, or 400 g (13 oz) can tomatoes
2 x 400 g (13 oz) cans butter beans, drained and rinsed
2 tablespoons chopped sage
pepper
crusty bread, to serve

Pour 300 ml (½ pint) of the stock into a large saucepan and add the fennel, onion, courgette, carrot and garlic. Cover the pan and bring to the boil. Boil for 5 minutes, then remove the lid, reduce the heat and simmer gently for 20 minutes, or until the vegetables are tender.

Stir in the tomatoes, beans and sage. Season to taste with pepper and pour in the remaining stock. Simmer for 5 minutes, then allow the soup to cool slightly.

Transfer 300 ml (½ pint) of the soup to a food processor or blender and whiz until smooth. Stir back into the pan and heat through gently. Pour into warmed bowls and serve with crusty bread.

NUTRITIONAL INFORMATION When choosing canned vegetables, go for the 'no added salt' varieties. If these aren't available, drain and rinse vegetables such as beans and sweetcorn. This removes some of the salt.

207 kcals (867 kj) ■ low fat ■ low GI ■ high fibre

19 Caldo verde

20 Spicy lentil and coriander soup

Preparation time:
10 minutes

Cooking time:
40 minutes

Serves: **6**

2 tablespoons olive oil
1 large onion, chopped
2 garlic cloves, chopped
500 g (1 lb) potatoes, peeled and cut into
  2.5 cm (1 inch) cubes
1.2 litres (2 pints) Vegetable Stock (see
  Introduction) or water
250 g (8 oz) spring greens, finely
  shredded
2 tablespoons chopped parsley
salt and pepper
breadsticks, to serve

Heat the oil in a large frying pan and fry the onion for 5 minutes until softened but not brown. Add the garlic and potatoes and cook for a few minutes, stirring occasionally.

Add the stock or water, season to taste with salt and pepper and cook for 15 minutes until the potatoes are tender. Mash the potatoes roughly in their liquid, then add the greens and boil uncovered for 10 minutes. Add the parsley and simmer for 2–3 minutes until heated through. Pour into warmed bowls and serve with breadsticks.

Preparation time:
15 minutes

Cooking time:
about 2¼ hours

Serves: **8**

500 g (1 lb) red lentils, well rinsed
2 tablespoons vegetable oil
2 onions, chopped
2 garlic cloves, chopped
2 celery sticks, chopped
400 g (13 oz) can tomatoes, drained
1 chilli, deseeded and chopped (optional)
1 teaspoon paprika
1 teaspoon harissa
1 teaspoon ground cumin
1.2 litres (2 pints) Vegetable Stock (see
  Introduction) or water
salt and pepper
2 tablespoons chopped coriander leaves,
  to garnish
crusty wholegrain bread, to serve
  (optional)

Put the lentils into a bowl of water. Heat the oil in a saucepan and gently fry the onions, garlic and celery over a low heat until softened.

Drain the lentils and add them to the saucepan with the tomatoes. Mix well. Add the chilli, if using, paprika, harissa, cumin and stock and season to taste with salt and pepper. Cover the pan and simmer gently for about 2 hours, adding a little more stock or water if the soup gets too thick.

Serve the soup immediately in warmed individual bowls with crusty wholegrain bread, if liked, and topped with a little chopped coriander.

NUTRITIONAL INFORMATION Leafy vegetables, including spring greens, are good sources of iron, vitamins A and C, potassium, calcium and fibre.

282 kcals (1185 kj) ■ low fat ■ high fibre ■ source of potassium ■ source of vitamins A and C

NUTRITIONAL INFORMATION The addition of lentils to this heartwarming soup creates a smooth creamy flavour, as well as contributing valuable iron and B vitamins.

599 kcals (2504 kj) ■ low GI ■ high fibre ■ source of iron ■ source of protein ■ source of vitamin B

21 Cauliflower and cumin soup

22 Red pepper and courgette soup

Preparation time:
15 minutes

Cooking time:
25 minutes

Serves: **4**

2 teaspoons oil
1 onion, chopped
1 garlic clove, crushed
2 teaspoons cumin seeds
1 cauliflower, cut into florets
1 large potato, peeled and chopped
450 ml (¾ pint) Vegetable Stock (see Introduction)
450 ml (¾ pint) semi-skimmed milk
2 tablespoons low-fat crème fraîche
2 tablespoons chopped coriander leaves
salt (optional) and pepper
crusty wholemeal bread, to serve (optional)

Preparation time:
15 minutes

Cooking time:
40 minutes

Serves: **4**

2 onions, finely chopped
2 tablespoons olive oil
1 garlic clove, crushed (optional)
3 red peppers, cored, deseeded and roughly chopped
2 courgettes, roughly chopped
900 ml (1½ pints) Vegetable Stock (see Introduction) or water
salt and pepper

TO SERVE:
low-fat natural yogurt or crème fraîche
whole chives

Heat the oil in a medium saucepan and fry the onion, garlic and cumin seeds for 3–4 minutes. Add the cauliflower, potato, stock and milk and bring to the boil. Reduce the heat and simmer for 15 minutes.

Transfer the soup to a food processor or blender and whiz until smooth. Stir through the crème fraîche and coriander and season to taste with salt, if liked, and pepper. Heat through and serve with crusty wholemeal bread, if liked.

Put the onions into a large saucepan with the oil and gently fry for 5 minutes, or until softened and golden brown. Add the garlic, if using, and cook gently for 1 minute. Add the peppers and half the courgettes to the pan. Fry for 5–8 minutes, or until softened and brown.

Add the stock to the pan, season to taste with salt and pepper and bring to the boil. Reduce the heat, cover the pan and simmer gently for 20 minutes.

When the vegetables are tender, allow the soup to cool slightly, then purée in batches in a food processor or blender. Return the soup to the pan. Season the soup to taste, then reheat and serve topped with the remaining chopped courgette, yogurt or crème fraîche and chives.

NUTRITIONAL INFORMATION Cauliflower is a source of glucosinates – phytochemicals that are believed to have strong anti-cancer effects by stimulating our natural defences.

401 kcals (1676 kj) ■ **low GI** ■ **source of protein**

NUTRITIONAL INFORMATION Red peppers are a very rich source of beta-carotene and vitamin C. They also contain the natural pain-killer capsaicin, which is clinically proven to be effective when rubbed on joints as a cream.

639 kcals (2671 kj) ■ **low GI** ■ **source of antioxidants** ■ **source of vitamin C**

23 Summer vegetable soup

24 Borscht with soured cream and chives

Preparation time:
15 minutes

Cooking time:
15 minutes

Serves: **4**

1 teaspoon olive oil
1 leek, finely sliced
1 large potato, peeled and chopped
450 g (14½ oz) mixed summer vegetables (such as peas, asparagus, broad beans and courgettes)
2 tablespoons chopped mint
900 ml (1½ pints) Vegetable Stock (see Introduction)
2 tablespoons low-fat crème fraîche
salt (optional) and pepper

Heat the oil in a medium saucepan and fry the leek for 3–4 minutes until softened.

Add all the remaining vegetables to the pan with the mint and stock and bring to the boil. Reduce the heat and simmer for 10 minutes.

Transfer the soup to a food processor or blender and whiz until smooth. Return the soup to the pan, add the crème fraîche and season to taste with salt, if liked, and pepper. Heat through gently and serve.

Preparation time:
25 minutes

Cooking time:
1 hour

Serves: **6**

750 g (1½ lb) raw beetroot, washed
1 carrot, peeled and grated
1 onion, grated
2 garlic cloves, crushed
1.5 litres (2½ pints) Vegetable Stock (see Introduction)
4 tablespoons lemon juice
2 tablespoons sugar
1 large cooked beetroot
salt and pepper

TO GARNISH:
150 ml (¼ pint) soured cream
1 teaspoon snipped chives
whole chives

Scrape young beetroot, or peel older ones, then coarsely grate the flesh into a large saucepan. Add the carrot, onion, garlic, stock, lemon juice and sugar and season to taste with salt and pepper. Bring to the boil. Reduce the heat, cover the pan and simmer for 45 minutes.

Meanwhile, cut the whole cooked beetroot into matchsticks about 3.5 cm (1½ inches) long. Cover and chill until required.

When the soup vegetables are tender, strain the contents of the pan through a muslin-lined sieve. Discard the vegetables.

Return the soup to the rinsed pan with the beetroot matchsticks. Bring gently to the boil, then simmer for a few minutes to warm the beetroot through. Season to taste with salt and pepper, ladle into warmed soup bowls and serve with a spoonful of soured cream, garnished with snipped chives and whole chives.

575 kcals (2404 kj) ■ **low GI** ■ **source of protein**

634 kcals (2650 kj) ■ **low fat** ■ **low GI** ■ **source of antioxidants** ■ **source of folic acid**

25 Butternut squash and rosemary soup

26 Watercress soup with yogurt

Preparation time:
15 minutes

Cooking time:
1 hour 10 minutes

Oven temperature:
200°C (400°F) Gas Mark 6

Serves: **4**

1 butternut squash
few rosemary sprigs, plus extra to garnish
150 g (5 oz) red lentils, well rinsed
1 onion, finely chopped
900 ml (1½ pints) Vegetable Stock (see Introduction)
salt and pepper
crusty white bread, to serve (optional)

Preparation time:
20 minutes

Cooking time:
20 minutes

Serves: **4**

25 g (1 oz) butter
1 small onion, finely chopped
100 g (3½ oz) watercress
2 tablespoons long-grain white rice
600 ml (1 pint) Chicken or Vegetable Stock (see Introduction)
300 ml (½ pint) semi-skimmed milk
150 g (5 oz) low-fat natural yogurt, plus 4 tablespoons to garnish
salt and pepper

Halve the squash, scoop out the seeds and fibrous flesh with a spoon and discard. Cut the squash into large chunks and put them into a roasting tin. Sprinkle with the rosemary, season to taste with salt and pepper and bake in a preheated oven, 200°C (400°F), Gas Mark 6, for 45 minutes.

Meanwhile, put the lentils into a large saucepan. Cover with water, bring to the boil and boil rapidly for 10 minutes. Drain the lentils, then return them to the rinsed pan with the onion and stock and simmer for 5 minutes. Season to taste with salt and pepper.

Remove the squash from the oven. Scoop out the flesh, mash it with a fork and add to the soup. Simmer the soup for 25 minutes, then ladle it into bowls. Garnish with more rosemary and serve with crusty white bread, if liked.

Heat the butter in a large saucepan and gently fry the onion for 5 minutes until softened.

Reserve a few sprigs of watercress for garnish and put them into a bowl of cold water. Tear the remaining watercress into pieces and add to the onion together with the rice, stock and salt and pepper to taste. Bring the stock to the boil, then reduce the heat, cover the pan and simmer for 10 minutes until the rice is tender but the watercress is still bright green.

Transfer the mixture to a food processor or blender and whiz until smooth. Return the mixture to the pan, stir in the milk and yogurt and heat gently for 2–3 minutes without boiling.

Ladle the soup into shallow soup bowls. Drop little dots of yogurt into each one with a teaspoon, then run a skewer through the dots to give a teardrop effect. Garnish with the reserved watercress leaves.

NUTRITIONAL INFORMATION Orange-fleshed squashes like the butternut squash used here are rich in carotenoids as well as other antioxidants, vitamins C and E.

180 kcals (752 kj) ■ low fat ■ source of antioxidants ■ source of vitamins C and E

180 kcals (752 kj) ■ low fat ■ low carb ■ source of calcium

27 Pea, lettuce and lemon soup

28 Tomato and orange soup with basil yogurt

Preparation time:
10 minutes

Cooking time:
20 minutes

Oven temperature:
200°C (400°F) Gas Mark 6

Serves: **4**

25 g (1 oz) butter
1 large onion, finely chopped
425 g (14 oz) frozen peas
2 Little Gem lettuces, roughly chopped
1 litre (1¾ pints) Vegetable or Chicken Stock (see Introduction)
grated rind and juice of ½ lemon
salt and pepper

SESAME CROUTONS:
2 thick slices of bread, cubed
1 tablespoon olive oil
1 tablespoon sesame seeds

To make the croûtons, brush the bread cubes with the oil and put into a roasting tin. Sprinkle with the sesame seeds and bake in a preheated oven, 200°C (400°F), Gas Mark 6, for 10–15 minutes, or until golden.

Meanwhile, heat the butter in a large saucepan and fry the onion for 5 minutes until softened. Add the peas, lettuce, stock, lemon rind and juice and salt and pepper to taste. Bring to the boil, then reduce the heat, cover the pan and simmer for 10–15 minutes.

Allow the soup to cool slightly, then transfer to a food processor or blender and whiz until smooth. Return the soup to the pan, adjust the seasoning if necessary and heat through. Spoon into warmed serving bowls and sprinkle with the sesame croûtons.

NUTRITIONAL INFORMATION Freezing peas has very little effect on their nutritional value. In fact, if frozen soon after harvesting, they usually contain more vitamin C than fresh peas.

806 kcals (3369 kj) ▪ **low GI** ▪ **high fibre** ▪ **source of vitamin C**

Preparation time:
15 minutes

Cooking time:
35–40 minutes

Serves: **6**

2 tablespoons olive oil
1 onion, roughly chopped
2 garlic cloves, crushed
2 kg (4 lb) ripe tomatoes, skinned and chopped
2 tablespoons tomato purée
450 ml (¾ pint) Vegetable or Chicken Stock (see Introduction)
grated rind of 1 large orange
75 ml (3 fl oz) orange juice
4 basil sprigs
1–2 teaspoons brown sugar
salt and pepper

TO GARNISH:
2–3 tablespoons finely chopped basil
150 ml (¼ pint) low-fat Greek yogurt
6 small basil sprigs
thin strips of orange rind

Heat the oil in a large saucepan and fry the onion and garlic until softened. Add the tomatoes, tomato purée, stock, orange rind and juice and basil. Bring to the boil, then reduce the heat, cover the pan and simmer gently for 20–25 minutes until the vegetables are soft.

Allow the soup to cool slightly, then purée in batches in a food processor or blender and push through a nylon sieve into the rinsed pan to remove the seeds. Season with salt, pepper and a little sugar. Return the pan to the heat and bring to the boil, then add a little extra stock or tomato juice if necessary to achieve the desired consistency.

To serve, fold the chopped basil gently into the Greek yogurt. Pour the hot soup into warmed soup plates, spoon a little basil yogurt on each one and top with small basil sprigs and orange rind.

129 kcals (545 kj) ▪ **low fat** ▪ **low GI** ▪ **source of antioxidants** ▪ **source of vitamin C**

29 Griddled vegetable soup 30 Courgette and dill soup

Preparation time:
15 minutes

Cooking time:
35–40 minutes

Serves: 4

1 red onion, sliced
**4 red peppers, cored, deseeded and cut
into flat pieces**
2 courgettes, sliced
1 aubergine, sliced
2 garlic cloves, sliced
400 ml (14 fl oz) tomato juice
**75 g (3 oz) Parmesan cheese, freshly
grated**
1 bunch of basil, chopped
6 tablespoons olive oil
salt and pepper

Heat a griddle pan. First, griddle all the vegetables as detailed below, then set aside. Griddle the onion slices for 5 minutes on each side. Griddle the pepper pieces for 6 minutes on the skin side only until charred and blistered. Remove the skin when cool enough to handle.

Griddle the courgette slices for 4 minutes on each side, the aubergine slices for 5 minutes on each side and the garlic slices for 1 minute on each side.

Transfer all the griddled vegetables to a food processor or blender, reserving a few slices of courgette, add the tomato juice and whiz until the soup is smooth or retains a little texture, according to your taste.

Put the grated Parmesan into a small bowl. Add the basil, oil and a little salt and pepper and mix well.

Taste the soup and adjust the seasoning if necessary. Serve it hot or cold, garnished with the reserved courgette slices and a little of the Parmesan and basil mixture just before serving. Serve the remainder separately at the table for guests to help themselves.

330 kcals (1379 kj) ▪ low carb ▪ low GI ▪ source of antioxidants ▪ source of vitamin C

Preparation time:
10 minutes

Cooking time:
30–40 minutes

Serves: 8

2–3 tablespoons olive oil
1 large onion, chopped
2 garlic cloves, crushed
1 kg (2 lb) courgettes, roughly chopped
**1.2–1.5 litres (2–2½ pints) Chicken Stock
(see Introduction)**
2–4 tablespoons finely chopped dill
salt and pepper

TO GARNISH:
2–4 tablespoons low-fat fromage frais
dill sprigs

Heat the oil in a saucepan and gently fry the onion and garlic until soft but not coloured. Add the courgettes and cook gently for 10–15 minutes until tender.

Add the stock, cover the pan and simmer for a further 10–15 minutes.

Transfer the courgettes and a little stock to a food processor or blender and whiz until smooth. Return to the pan and bring to the boil with the remaining stock, the dill and salt and pepper to taste.

Serve the soup in warmed bowls, garnished with swirls of fromage frais and dill sprigs.

COOK'S NOTES This soup is excellent served chilled and can be frozen for up to 3 months. After defrosting, it will improve the texture if you whiz it in a food processor or blender before garnishing and serving.

95 kcals (397 kj) ▪ low fat ▪ low carb ▪ low GI

31 Red pepper and ginger soup

32 Fragrant tofu and noodle soup

Preparation time:
20 minutes, plus cooling

Cooking time:
45 minutes

Oven temperature:
200°C (400°F) Gas Mark 6

Serves: **4**

3 red peppers, halved, cored and
   deseeded
1 red onion, quartered
2 garlic cloves, unpeeled
1 teaspoon olive oil
5 cm (2 inch) piece of fresh root ginger,
   peeled and grated
1 teaspoon ground cumin
1 teaspoon ground coriander
1 large potato, peeled and chopped
900 ml (1½ pints) Vegetable Stock (see
   Introduction)
salt and pepper
4 tablespoons low-fat fromage frais,
   to garnish

Preparation time:
15 minutes, plus draining

Cooking time:
10 minutes

Serves: **2**

125 g (4 oz) firm tofu, diced
1 tablespoon sesame oil
75 g (3 oz) thin dried rice noodles
600 ml (1 pint) Vegetable Stock (see
   Introduction)
2.5 cm (1 inch) piece of fresh root ginger,
   peeled and thickly sliced
1 large garlic clove, thickly sliced
3 kaffir lime leaves, torn in half
2 lemon grass stalks, halved
handful of spinach or pak choi leaves
50 g (2 oz) bean sprouts
1–2 fresh red chillies, deseeded and
   finely sliced
2 tablespoons coriander leaves
1 tablespoon Thai fish sauce

TO SERVE:
lime wedges
chilli sauce

Put the peppers, onion and garlic cloves into a nonstick roasting tin and roast in a preheated oven, 200°C (400°F), Gas 6, for 40 minutes, or until the peppers have blistered.

Meanwhile, heat the oil in a saucepan and gently fry the ginger, cumin and coriander for 5 minutes. Add the potato, stir well and season to taste with salt and pepper. Pour in the stock and simmer, covered, for 30 minutes.

When cool enough to handle, pop the garlic cloves out of their skins and pulp them. Add the onion and garlic to the potato mixture. Skin the peppers and add all but one half to the soup. Simmer for 5 minutes.

Transfer the soup to a food processor or blender and whiz until smooth. Return to the pan and reheat. Cut the reserved pepper into thin strips. Pour the soup into warmed bowls and garnish with fromage frais and the strips of red pepper.

Put the tofu on a plate lined with kitchen paper and allow to stand for 10 minutes to drain.

Heat the oil in a wok until hot and stir-fry the tofu for 2–3 minutes, or until golden brown. Drain the tofu on kitchen paper.

Meanwhile, soak the noodles in boiling water for 2 minutes, then drain.

Pour the stock into a large saucepan. Add the ginger, garlic, lime leaves and lemon grass and bring to the boil. Reduce the heat, add the tofu, noodles, spinach or pak choi, bean sprouts and chillies and heat through. Add the coriander and fish sauce, then pour into deep bowls. Serve with lime wedges and chilli sauce.

588 kcals (2476 kj) ■ **low fat** ■ **low GI** ■ **source of antioxidants** ■ **source of vitamin C**

294 kcals (1172 kj) ■ **low GI** ■ **source of protein** ■ **source of vitamin B**

33 Prawn and noodle soup 34 Prawn and lime soup

Preparation time: **10 minutes**	**900 ml (1½ pints) Vegetable or Chicken** **Stock (see Introduction)** **2 kaffir lime leaves**
Cooking time: **15 minutes**	**1 lemon grass stalk, lightly bruised** **150 g (5 oz) dried egg noodles** **50 g (2 oz) frozen peas**
Serves: **4**	**50 g (2 oz) frozen sweetcorn kernels** **100 g (3½ oz) large king prawns, cooked,** **peeled and deveined** **4 spring onions, sliced** **2 teaspoons soy sauce**

Preparation time: **15 minutes**	**5 red chillies** **6 kaffir lime leaves** **1 string of green peppercorns**
Cooking time: **20 minutes**	**1 lemon grass stalk, finely sliced** **1 litre (1¾ pints) water** **2 tablespoons Thai fish sauce**
Serves: **4**	**2 tablespoons sugar** **500 g (1 lb) raw king prawns, peeled and** **deveined** **4 tablespoons lime juice** **handful of coriander leaves**

Put the stock into a saucepan with the lime leaves and lemon grass, bring to the boil, then reduce the heat and simmer for 10 minutes.

Add the noodles to the stock and cook according to the packet instructions. After 2 minutes, add the peas, sweetcorn, prawns, spring onions and soy sauce. Serve in warmed bowls.

Put the chillies, kaffir lime leaves, peppercorns, lemon grass and measurement water into a large saucepan. Bring slowly to the boil and boil for 10 minutes. Reduce the heat and add the fish sauce and sugar.

When the soup has reached a simmer, add the prawns and simmer gently until they have turned pink. Remove the pan from the heat and add the lime juice and coriander leaves. Serve the soup immediately.

NUTRITIONAL INFORMATION Limes are rich in vitamin C and bioflavonoids. Pure lime juice has powerful antibacterial properties and is an effective treatment when applied directly to spots and cold sores.

206 kcals (863 kj) ■ **low fat** ■ **low GI**

181 kcals (761 kj) ■ **low fat** ■ **low carb** ■ **low GI** ■
source of bioflavonoids ■ **source of vitamin C**

Preparation time:
15 minutes

Cooking time:
about 25 minutes

Serves: **4**

1.2 litres (2 pints) Chicken Stock (see Introduction)
2 tablespoons light soy sauce, plus extra to serve (optional)
1 tablespoon vinegar
1 tablespoon medium dry sherry
250 g (8 oz) lean pork fillet, cut diagonally into 3.5 x 1 cm (1½ x ½ inch) strips
3 spring onions, diagonally sliced
2.5 cm (1 inch) piece of fresh root ginger, peeled and cut into very fine matchsticks
125 g (4 oz) button mushrooms, thinly sliced
200 g (7 oz) Chinese leaves, shredded
125 g (4 oz) bean sprouts
125 g (4 oz) medium dried egg noodles
salt and pepper

Pour the stock into a large saucepan and bring it to the boil. Add the soy sauce, vinegar, sherry, pork strips, spring onions, ginger and mushrooms. Stir once, then cover the pan and simmer for 10 minutes, stirring occasionally.

Add the Chinese leaves and cook for 5 minutes. Add the bean sprouts and noodles and season to taste with salt and pepper. Cook for a further 5 minutes, or until the noodles are tender. Taste and adjust the seasoning if necessary. Serve with some extra soy sauce, if liked.

NUTRITIONAL INFORMATION Oriental soups are very nutritious, as the vegetables are cooked for the minimum of time, retaining vitamins as well as colour and crunch.

380 kcals (1597 kj) ■ **low fat** ■ **low GI**

Preparation time:
10 minutes, plus chilling (optional)

Cooking time:
8–10 minutes

Serves: **6**

300 g (10 oz) can condensed cream of celery soup
300 ml (½ pint) semi-skimmed milk
½ teaspoon paprika, or to taste
½ teaspoon white pepper
2 tablespoons low-fat natural yogurt
50 g (2 oz) cooked peeled prawns, defrosted if frozen
snipped chives, to garnish

Mix together the celery soup and milk in a saucepan. Add the paprika a little at a time, to taste, and white pepper. Bring to simmering point, stirring constantly, and simmer for 5 minutes, then remove the pan from the heat.

To serve the soup hot, stir in the yogurt and prawns and reheat gently for about 2 minutes. Do not allow to boil. Serve in warmed bowls and garnish each portion with snipped chives.

To serve the soup chilled, pour it into a bowl and leave to cool. Stir in the yogurt and prawns, then cover and chill for at least 3 hours. Serve the soup in chilled bowls, garnished with snipped chives.

64 kcals (268 kj) ■ **low fat** ■ **low carb**

3 Starters

37 Baked field mushrooms

38 Potato wedges with yogurt and parsley dip

Preparation time:
5 minutes

Cooking time:
40 minutes

Oven temperature:
200°C (400°F) Gas Mark 6

Serves: **4**

5 large field or open-cap mushrooms
4 tablespoons balsamic vinegar
1 tablespoon wholegrain mustard
75 g (3 oz) watercress
salt and pepper
**Parmesan cheese shavings, to garnish
 (optional)**

Remove the stalks from 4 of the mushrooms and reserve. Put the 4 mushrooms into a small roasting tin, skin side down, and cook in a preheated oven, 200°C (400°F), Gas Mark 6, for 15 minutes.

Meanwhile, to make the dressing, finely chop the remaining mushroom and the reserved stalks and mix with the vinegar and mustard in a small bowl. Season to taste with salt and pepper.

Remove the mushrooms from the oven and spoon the dressing over them. Return the mushrooms to the oven and continue to cook for 25 minutes, covering the tin with a piece of foil after 10 minutes.

Lift the mushrooms on to a plate with a slotted spoon and keep them warm. Tip the watercress into the hot juices and toss well. Divide the watercress between 4 warmed plates, put a mushroom on top and garnish with Parmesan shavings, if liked.

Preparation time:
10 minutes

Cooking time:
about 15 minutes

Serves: **1**

1 potato, about 175 g (6 oz)
1 red pepper, cored, deseeded and sliced
1 teaspoon olive oil
paprika, to taste
salt

YOGURT AND PARSLEY DIP:
3 tablespoons low-fat natural yogurt
1 tablespoon chopped parsley
2 spring onions, chopped
1 garlic clove, crushed (optional)
salt and pepper

Cut the potato into 8 wedges and cook them in a saucepan of lightly salted boiling water for 5 minutes. Drain the wedges thoroughly, then put them into a bowl with the pepper slices and toss with the oil. Sprinkle with paprika and salt to taste.

Arrange the potato wedges and pepper slices on a baking sheet and cook under a preheated hot grill for 6–8 minutes, turning occasionally, until cooked.

Meanwhile, to make the yogurt and parsley dip, put the yogurt, parsley, spring onions and garlic, if using, into a bowl. Season to taste with salt and pepper and mix thoroughly.

Serve the potato wedges and pepper slices hot with the yogurt dip.

39 kcals (165 kj) ▪ **low fat** ▪ **low carb** ▪ **low GI** ▪
source of iron ▪ **source of potassium**

260 kcals (1097 kj) ▪ **low fat** ▪ **source of calcium** ▪
source of vitamin A

39 Fresh figs with ricotta and parma ham

Preparation time:	8 fresh figs
10 minutes	**1 teaspoon Dijon mustard**
	125 g (4 oz) ricotta cheese
Serves: **4**	**85 g (3¼ oz) Parma ham**
	2 tablespoons balsamic vinegar
	salt and pepper

Cut the figs into quarters, leaving them attached at the base. Stir the mustard into the ricotta and season to taste with salt and pepper.

Divide the ricotta mixture between the figs, spooning it over the top. Put 2 figs on each serving plate and top with some Parma ham. Serve drizzled with the vinegar.

NUTRITIONAL INFORMATION Figs can be part of almost any special diet – low-fat, low-sodium, high-fibre, calorie-controlled or diabetic. They are fat-, sodium- and cholesterol-free, while having a satisfying sweetness.

200 kcals (838 kj) ■ **low fat** ■ **low GI** ■ **high fibre** ■ **source of antioxidants**

40 Aubergine, tomato and mozzarella mountains

Preparation time:	1 aubergine, cut into 8 slices
10 minutes	**2 beef tomatoes, skinned and cut into 8 slices**
Cooking time:	**175 g (6 oz) buffalo mozzarella cheese, cut into 8 slices**
20 minutes	**1 tablespoon olive oil, plus extra for oiling**
Oven temperature:	**salt and pepper**
190°C (375°F) Gas Mark 5	**mint sprigs, to garnish**
Serves: **4**	**4 tablespoons ready-made fresh pesto, to serve**

Cook the aubergine slices under a preheated hot grill, turning occasionally, until browned on both sides.

Put 4 of the aubergine slices on an oiled baking sheet. Put a tomato slice and a mozzarella slice on each one, then make a second layer of aubergine, tomato and mozzarella, sprinkling with a little salt and pepper as you go. Skewer each stack with a cocktail stick to hold them together.

Bake the stacks in a preheated oven, 190°C (375°F), Gas Mark 5, for 10 minutes.

Transfer the stacks to warmed plates and remove the cocktail sticks. Drizzle with a little oil and top with a generous spoonful of pesto. Serve warm or at room temperature, garnished with mint sprigs.

247 kcals (1033 kj) ■ **low carb** ■ **low GI** ■ **source of antioxidants** ■ **source of vitamin C**

41 Tomato bruschetta

42 Smoked salmon blinis with dill cream

Preparation time:
5 minutes

Cooking time:
about 10 minutes

Serves: **1**

12 cherry tomatoes
50 g (2 oz) mozzarella cheese
3 slices of ciabatta
olive oil, for brushing
few basil leaves

Preparation time:
5 minutes

Cooking time:
5 minutes

Serves: **4**

8 large blinis
2 tablespoons low-fat crème fraîche
1 teaspoon chopped dill
grated rind of 1 lemon
2 spring onions, sliced
100 g (3½ oz) smoked salmon strips
pepper

TO GARNISH:
thin strips of lemon rind
lemon wedges

Chop the cherry tomatoes into small pieces and thinly slice the mozzarella. Set aside.

Toast the ciabatta lightly on both sides, then brush one side with a little oil and arrange the mozzarella and chopped cherry tomatoes on top. Tear the basil leaves into small pieces and scatter over the bruschetta.

Cook the bruschetta under a preheated hot grill until the cheese has melted slightly. Serve immediately.

Gently warm the blinis for a few minutes under a preheated grill or in a preheated oven.

Stir together the crème fraîche, dill, lemon rind and spring onions and season to taste with pepper. Spoon the mixture on to the blinis and top with the smoked salmon. Garnish with lemon rind and wedges and serve immediately.

NUTRITIONAL INFORMATION Low-fat crème fraîche is lower in fat than single cream and has only a third of the fat of standard crème fraîche. It's the smart choice for a low-fat diet.

269 kcals (1126 kj) ■ **low fat** ■ **source of antioxidants** ■ **source of calcium**

159 kcals (667 kj) ■ **low fat** ■ **low carb** ■ **low GI** ■ **source of omega-3 fatty acids**

43 Aubergine and red pepper layer toasts

Preparation time:
20 minutes, plus standing

Cooking time:
about 15 minutes

Serves: **4**

1 small aubergine
1 tablespoon olive oil
2 large red peppers, cored, deseeded and quartered
4 large slices of day-old wholemeal bread
1 garlic clove, peeled and halved
1 ripe tomato, halved
125 g (4 oz) goats' cheese
pepper
flat leaf parsley sprigs, to garnish

Cut the aubergine into 5 mm (¼ inch) thick slices, brush with a little of the oil and put them on a grill rack. Cook under a preheated hot grill for 2–3 minutes on each side until charred and tender. Remove and allow to cool.

Grill the pepper quarters, skin side up, until the skins are charred. Transfer to a polythene bag and leave to soften for 15 minutes.

Meanwhile, toast the bread on both sides and immediately rub it all over with the cut sides of garlic and then the cut sides of the tomato. Brush with any remaining oil.

Remove and discard the charred pepper skins and cut the flesh into wide strips. Layer the aubergine and peppers over the toast. Cut the goats' cheese into 4 slices and put a slice on each piece of toast. Season to taste with pepper. Return the toasts to the grill for 1–2 minutes until the cheese is bubbling and melted. Garnish with the parsley and serve immediately.

243 kcals (1022 kj) ▪ **low GI** ▪ **high fibre** ▪ **source of antioxidants**

44 Vietnamese salad rolls with dipping sauce

Preparation time:
15 minutes

Serves: **4**

12 small rice-paper spring roll wrappers
1 carrot, cut into fine julienne
1 cucumber, halved lengthways, deseeded and cut into fine julienne
125 g (4 oz) enoki mushrooms, trimmed and sliced
2 spring onions, finely shredded
15 g (½ oz) mint leaves, chopped
15 g (½ oz) coriander leaves, chopped

DIPPING SAUCE:
2 tablespoons Vietnamese fish sauce
3 tablespoons lime juice
2 teaspoons caster sugar
1 small red chilli, finely sliced

Soak the spring roll wrappers in hot water for 1–2 minutes until soft. Drain well, then cover with a damp tea towel.

Divide the carrot, cucumber, mushrooms, spring onions, mint and coriander between the wrappers. Fold and roll the wrappers around the salad filling to enclose it neatly. Cover with a damp tea towel until ready to serve.

Mix together all the ingredients for the dipping sauce in a small bowl. Arrange the salad rolls on a platter and serve with the sauce.

NUTRITIONAL INFORMATION Chillies owe their heat to the phytochemical capsaicin, which is concentrated in the seeds and can help relieve nasal congestion. They are also rich in vitamin C.

136 kcals (569 kj) ▪ **low fat** ▪ **low GI** ▪ **source of potassium** ▪ **source of vitamin C**

45 Aubergine pâté

46 Butter bean, anchovy and coriander pâté

Preparation time:	25 g (1 oz) dried porcini mushrooms
10 minutes, plus soaking	**500 g (1 lb) aubergines**
	6 tablespoons olive oil
Cooking time:	**1 small red onion, chopped**
15 minutes	**2 teaspoons cumin seeds**
	175 g (6 oz) cup or chestnut mushrooms
	2 garlic cloves, crushed
Serves: **6**	**3 pickled walnuts, halved**
	small handful of coriander leaves
	salt and pepper
	thick slices of white bread, to serve

Put the dried mushrooms into a heatproof bowl and cover with plenty of boiling water. Leave to soak for 10 minutes.

Meanwhile, cut the aubergines into 1 cm (½ inch) dice. Heat the oil in a large frying pan and gently fry the aubergines and onion for 8 minutes until the vegetables are soft and browned.

Drain the dried mushrooms and add to the pan with the cumin seeds, fresh mushrooms and garlic. Fry for 5–7 minutes until the aubergines are very soft.

Transfer the mixture to a food processor or blender with the pickled walnuts and coriander, season to taste with salt and pepper and whiz to a rough paste. Transfer the pâté to a serving dish and serve warm or cold with white bread.

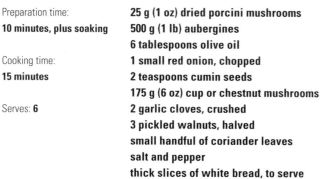

Preparation time:	425 g (14 oz) can butter beans, drained
5–10 minutes	**and rinsed**
	50 g (2 oz) can anchovy fillets in oil,
Serves: **3**	**drained**
	2 spring onions, finely chopped
	2 tablespoons lemon juice
	1 tablespoon olive oil
	4 tablespoons chopped coriander leaves
	salt and pepper
	toasted rye bread, to serve

Put the butter beans, anchovies, spring onions, lemon juice and oil into a food processor or blender and whiz until well mixed but not smooth. Alternatively, mash the beans with a fork, finely chop the anchovies and mix the ingredients together by hand.

Stir in the coriander leaves and season well with salt and pepper. Serve the pâté with toasted rye bread.

COOK'S NOTES Use other canned beans for this pâté in place of the butter beans, such as cannellini or red kidney beans, if liked.

295 kcals (1239 kj) ▪ low carb ▪ low GI ▪ source of antioxidants ▪ source of potassium

190 kcals (799 kj) ▪ low GI ▪ high fibre ▪ source of protein

47 Hummus with roasted vegetables in tortillas

48 Red pepper and spring onion dip

Preparation time:
15 minutes

Cooking time:
45 minutes

Oven temperature:
200°C (400°F) Gas Mark 6

Serves: **4**

**400 g (13 oz) can chickpeas, rinsed and
    drained**
1 garlic clove
2 tablespoons Greek yogurt
juice of 1 lemon
pinch of paprika
1 aubergine, cut into batons
1 red pepper, cored, deseeded and sliced
2 courgettes, sliced
2 carrots, cut into batons
1 red onion, sliced
1 tablespoon olive oil
1 teaspoon chopped thyme
8 small flour tortillas

Preparation time:
10 minutes

Cooking time:
30–40 minutes

Oven temperature:
220°C (425°F) Gas Mark 7

Serves: **4**

**1 large red pepper, cored, deseeded and
    quartered**
2 garlic cloves, unpeeled
250 g (8 oz) low-fat natural yogurt
2 spring onions, finely chopped
pepper
**selection of raw vegetables, such as
    carrot, cucumber, pepper, fennel,
    tomato, baby corn cobs, mangetout,
    celery and courgette, cut into batons or
    slices, to serve**

To make the hummus, put the chickpeas, garlic clove, yogurt, lemon juice and paprika into a food processor or blender and whiz until smooth. Tip into a bowl, cover and set aside.

Arrange the vegetables in a roasting tin, drizzle with the oil and sprinkle with the thyme. Cook in a preheated oven, 200°C (400°F), Gas Mark 6, for 45 minutes until they are tender and beginning to char.

Meanwhile, warm the tortillas according to the packet instructions, then fill with the roasted vegetables and hummus and serve.

Slightly flatten the pepper quarters and put on a baking sheet. Wrap the garlic cloves in foil and add to the sheet. Roast in a preheated oven, 220°C (425°F), Gas Mark 7, for 30–40 minutes until the pepper is slightly charred and the garlic is soft.

When the pepper is cool enough to handle, remove the skin and discard. Transfer the flesh to a bowl. Squeeze the roasted garlic flesh from the cloves into the bowl and discard the skin.

Using a fork, roughly mash the pepper and garlic together. Stir in the yogurt and spring onions and season to taste with pepper. Serve with the vegetable batons and slices.

NUTRITIONAL INFORMATION Chickpeas are an excellent source of soluble fibre, which can help to lower blood cholesterol. They also provide folate, vitamin E, potassium, iron, manganese, copper, zinc and calcium, and as a high-potassium, low-sodium food, they help to reduce blood pressure.

564 kcals (2370 kj) ▪ **low GI** ▪ **high fibre** ▪ **source of antioxidants** ▪ **source of protein**

52 kcals (216 kj) ▪ **low fat** ▪ **low carb** ▪ **low GI** ▪ **source of antioxidants**

49 Griddled courgettes with lemon pesto

Preparation time:
10 minutes

Cooking time:
12 minutes

Serves: **4**

200 g (7 oz) baby courgettes
thin strips of lemon rind, to garnish (optional)

LEMON PESTO:
75 g (3 oz) pine nuts
1 large bunch of basil, roughly chopped
2 garlic cloves, crushed
75 g (3 oz) Parmesan cheese, freshly grated
grated rind and juice of 2 lemons
4 tablespoons olive oil
salt and pepper

TO SERVE:
griddled pitta bread
lemon wedges

Heat a griddle pan. Slice the courgettes in half lengthways, put a batch on the griddle and cook for 3 minutes on each side. Remove and keep warm while you griddle the remaining courgettes.

Meanwhile, to make the lemon pesto, heat a dry frying pan until hot, add the pine nuts and toast lightly, shaking the pan frequently. Whiz the basil, toasted pine nuts, garlic, Parmesan, lemon rind and juice, oil and salt and pepper to taste in a food processor or blender until smooth.

Arrange the griddled courgettes on a serving plate or 4 individual plates. Drizzle the lemon pesto over the top and serve garnished with lemon rind, if liked, and accompanied by griddled pitta bread and lemon wedges, for squeezing.

357 kcals (1492 kj) ▪ low carb ▪ low GI ▪ high fibre ▪ source of protein ▪ source of vitamin C

50 Griddled chicory with Parmesan

Preparation time:
5 minutes

Cooking time:
about 25 minutes

Serves: **4**

4 chicory heads
100 g (3½ oz) Parmesan cheese, freshly grated
salt and pepper
salad leaves, to serve

Heat a griddle pan. Slice the chicory heads in half lengthways, put a batch on the griddle and cook for 5 minutes on each side. Remove and keep warm while you griddle the remaining chicory.

Put the griddled chicory into an ovenproof dish, season to taste with salt and pepper and sprinkle with the grated Parmesan. Cook under a preheated grill until the Parmesan is just bubbling. Serve immediately, accompanied by salad leaves.

NUTRITIONAL INFORMATION Griddling is a healthy way to cook, since it requires little or no added fat, and any fat from the food can drain away. Griddle pans can be heated to a very high heat, which gives food a delicious flavour and helps to seal in all the juices.

119 kcals (497 kj) ▪ low fat ▪ low carb ▪ source of calcium

51 Griddled potatoes with wasabi sauce

52 Griddled fennel and onions

Preparation time:
10 minutes, plus standing

Cooking time:
40 minutes

Serves: **4**

750 g (1½ lb) new potatoes
5 tablespoons low-fat mayonnaise
3 tablespoons water
wasabi paste, to taste
salt

Heat a griddle pan. Cut the potatoes in half lengthways. Put a batch on the griddle and cook for 10 minutes on each side. When they are almost soft, remove them from the griddle, put them into a dish and leave to stand for 10 minutes to steam in their skins. Sprinkle with a little salt. Repeat with the remaining potatoes.

Blend the mayonnaise, measurement water and a little wasabi paste in a small bowl and serve with the potatoes.

Preparation time:
10 minutes

Cooking time:
25 minutes

Serves: **4**

2 red onions
2 fennel bulbs
2 teaspoons Dijon mustard
4 tablespoons lemon juice
5 tablespoons olive oil
salt and pepper

TO GARNISH:
thin strips of lemon rind
chopped basil

Heat a griddle pan. Cut the red onions into wedges, keeping the root ends intact to hold the wedges together. Put on the griddle and cook for 6 minutes on each side. Set aside.

Cut the fennel bulbs into quarters and remove the hard cores. Slice them roughly, then griddle for 6 minutes on each side.

Combine the mustard and lemon juice in a small bowl. Add the oil and mix well.

Put the griddled fennel and onions into a serving dish, season to taste with salt and pepper and pour over the dressing. Garnish with lemon rind and chopped basil and serve.

NUTRITIONAL INFORMATION Fresh potatoes contain much more vitamin C than those that have been stored. Potatoes should be cooked in their skins or peeled just before cooking, and should never be left soaking in water, as this causes them to lose vitamin C.

191 kcals (798 kj) ■ **low fat** ■ **high fibre** ■ **source of potassium** ■ **source of protein** ■ **source of vitamin C**

NUTRITIONAL INFORMATION Onions are from the same family as garlic with several probable medicinal benefits. Many experts believe that they can help to lower blood cholesterol and blood pressure, and thin blood to minimize the risk of clotting.

205 kcals (857 kj) ■ **low carb** ■ **low GI** ■ **source of antioxidants**

53 Greek stuffed vine leaves

Preparation time:
15 minutes

Cooking time:
30 minutes

Serves: **4**

425 g (14 oz) can vine leaves
2 tablespoons olive oil
150 g (5 oz) lean minced beef
1 large onion, finely chopped
¼ fennel bulb, grated
2 garlic cloves, crushed
150 g (5 oz) cooked long-grain brown rice
1 tablespoon chopped dill
1 teaspoon dried oregano
150 ml (¼ pint) dry red wine
150 ml (¼ pint) water
4 tablespoons lemon juice
salt and pepper
lemon wedges, to serve

Put the vine leaves into a sieve, rinse under cold running water and drain thoroughly.

Heat half the oil in a large frying pan and fry the mince, onion, fennel and garlic, stirring, until cooked. This will take about 8–10 minutes. Stir in the rice, dill and oregano and season to taste with salt and pepper.

Spread the mixture evenly over the vine leaves. Fold the long sides of the vine leaves over to secure the mixture and roll up securely from the shorter edge to make neat parcels.

Mix together the remaining oil, the wine, water and lemon juice in a saucepan. Add the stuffed vine leaves, cover the pan and cook over a gentle heat for about 20 minutes. Remove with a slotted spoon and serve with lemon wedges.

233 kcals (974 kj) ▪ **low GI** ▪ **high fibre** ▪ **source of iron** ▪ **source of vitamin B**

54 Crab and chicken parcels

Preparation time:
15 minutes, plus chilling

Cooking time:
15–20 minutes

Oven temperature:
190°C (375°F) Gas Mark 5

Makes: **8**

175 g (6 oz) cooked white crabmeat, drained if canned
125 g (4 oz) cooked chicken, minced
1 garlic clove, crushed
2 spring onions, chopped
1 tablespoon chopped coriander leaves
2 teaspoons chopped preserved stem ginger, plus 2 teaspoons jar syrup
¼ teaspoon chilli powder
1 tablespoon light soy sauce
grated rind and juice of 1 lime
8 x 10 cm (4 inch) wonton wrappers
2 tablespoons olive oil, plus extra for brushing and oiling
1 spring onion, shredded, to garnish
sweet and sour dipping sauce, to serve

Put all the ingredients, except the wonton wrappers and oil, into a bowl and stir well until combined. Cover and chill for 1 hour to allow the flavours to develop.

Brush each of the wonton wrappers with oil and put a spoonful of the crab mixture at one edge. Roll up loosely, tucking in the ends. Put the parcels on an oiled baking sheet, brush them with oil and bake in a preheated oven, 190°C (375°F), Gas Mark 5, for 15–20 minutes until golden and crisp. Serve the parcels hot with the dipping sauce, garnished with the spring onion.

NUTRITIONAL INFORMATION Shellfish such as squid, crab, prawns, lobster, mussels, clams, cockles and scallops are low in fat, rich in minerals and provide protein. Crabmeat contains significant amounts of omega-3 fatty acids.

(per parcel) 87 kcals (364 kj) ▪ **low fat** ▪ **low carb** ▪ **source of protein** ▪ **source of omega-3 fatty acids**

55 Mongolian lamb fondue

56 Herby polenta wedges with tomato salsa

Preparation time:
15 minutes

Cooking time:
15 minutes, plus about 10 minutes at the table

Serves: **4**

750 g (1½ lb) lean lamb fillet, sliced paper thin (this is easier to do if the lamb is partially frozen)
1.5 litres (2½ pints) Chicken Stock (see Introduction)
2.5 cm (1 inch) piece of fresh root ginger, peeled and cut into fine strips
1 garlic clove, finely sliced
4 tablespoons Chinese rice wine or dry sherry
2 tablespoons Thai fish sauce
6 spring onions, thinly sliced
500 g (1 lb) spinach
1 bunch of coriander, roughly chopped
250 g (8 oz) dried rice vermicelli noodles
selection of dipping sauces, to serve

Arrange the lamb slices on a large serving platter, cover and set aside. Simmer the stock in a saucepan with the ginger, garlic, wine and fish sauce for 15 minutes.

Pour the stock into a Mongolian hotpot or a fondue pot and stir in half the spring onions, spinach and coriander. Put the pot on its tabletop burner and return to the boil.

Using chopsticks (or fondue forks), each diner dips a slice of lamb into the stock to cook, then dips it into the dipping sauce. When the meat is finished, add the remaining greens and the noodles to the hotpot and cook for 5–10 minutes. When the noodles are tender, serve as a soup in individual bowls.

Preparation time:
10 minutes, plus setting

Cooking time:
15–20 minutes

Serves: **4**

75 g (3 oz) instant polenta or cornmeal
500 ml (17 fl oz) simmering water
75 g (3 oz) butter
40 g (1 ½ oz) Parmesan cheese, freshly grated
6 tablespoons chopped herbs, such as chervil, chives and parsley
salt and pepper

SPICY CHERRY TOMATO SALSA
10 oz ripe cherry tomatoes, quartered
2 red chillies, seeded and finely chopped
1 small red onion, finely chopped
2 tablespoons chilli oil
2 tablespoons olive oil
2 tablespoons lime juice
2 tablespoons shredded mint

Pour the polenta into a pan of the simmering measurement water and beat with a wooden spoon until it is thick and smooth. Reduce the heat and continue stirring for about 5 minutes, or according to the packet instructions, until cooked. Remove the pan from the heat, add the butter, Parmesan and herbs and stir until well combined. Season to taste with salt and pepper, then turn into a greased 25 cm (10 inch) pizza or cake tin, at least 2.5 cm (1 inch) deep. Smooth the top with the back of a spoon and leave to set for about 5–10 minutes.

Combine all the salsa ingredients in a bowl and season with salt and pepper to taste. Set aside.

Remove the set polenta from the tin and cut it into 8 wedges. Heat a griddle pan. Put the wedges on the griddle and cook for 2–3 minutes on each side until heated through and golden. Serve with the salsa.

745 kcals (3114 kj) ▪ **low GI** ▪ **source of iron** ▪ **source of protein**

414 kcals (1731 kj) ▪ **low GI** ▪ **source of antioxidants** ▪ **source of vitamin C**

57 Asparagus with tarragon and lemon dressing

58 Chilli-marinated butternut squash

Preparation time:
15 minutes

Cooking time:
about 5 minutes

Serves: **4**

3 tablespoons olive oil (optional)
500 g (1 lb) asparagus, trimmed
125 g (4 oz) rocket or other salad leaves
2 spring onions, finely sliced
4 radishes, finely sliced
salt and pepper

TARRAGON AND LEMON DRESSING:
2 tablespoons tarragon vinegar
finely grated rind of 1 lemon
¼ teaspoon Dijon mustard
pinch of sugar
1 tablespoon chopped tarragon
5 tablespoons olive oil or
grapeseed oil
salt and pepper

TO GARNISH:
roughly chopped herbs (such as tarragon,
parsley, chervil and dill)
thin strips of lemon rind

To make the dressing, mix together all the ingredients.

Heat the oil, if using, in a griddle pan. Put the asparagus in a single layer on the griddle and cook for about 5 minutes, turning occasionally – it should be tender when pierced with a knife and lightly patched with brown. Transfer it to a shallow dish and sprinkle with salt and pepper to taste. Cover with the dressing and toss gently, then allow to stand for 5 minutes.

Arrange the rocket or other salad leaves on a platter, sprinkle the spring onions and radishes over the top and arrange the asparagus in a pile in the middle. Garnish with chopped herbs and lemon rind.

Preparation time:
15 minutes, plus
marinating

Cooking time:
22 minutes

Serves: **4**

1 small butternut squash, peeled and cut
into thin wedges
1 red onion, cut into quarters
1 red pepper, cored, deseeded and cut
into thick strips
8 thin slices of chorizo sausage
lime juice, to serve

CHILLI MARINADE:
2–4 red chillies (depending on the heat
desired), deseeded and finely chopped
2 garlic cloves, crushed
1 wide strip of lemon rind
1 bay leaf, torn
50 ml (2 fl oz) olive oil
2 tablespoons cider vinegar
2 tablespoons lime juice
salt and pepper

Thoroughly mix together all the ingredients for the marinade in a large bowl and add the butternut squash, onion and pepper. Toss well, then cover and set aside at room temperature for about 1 hour.

Heat a griddle pan over a medium heat. Put the chorizo slices on the griddle and cook for 1 minute on each side until crisp. Remove and drain on kitchen paper.

Shake off any excess marinade from the butternut squash wedges, then griddle them for about 20 minutes, turning once. Add the pepper and onion for the last 3–4 minutes so that they char lightly.

Serve the butternut squash immediately, sprinkled with the chorizo and a squeeze of lime juice.

139 kcals (581 kj) ▪ low carb ▪ low GI ▪ source of antioxidants ▪ source of vitamin E

200 kcals (836 kj) ▪ low carb ▪ source of antioxidants

59 Broccoli and spinach eggah

Preparation time: **15 minutes**	**125 g (4 oz) broccoli** **100 g (3½ oz) baby spinach** **6 eggs**
Cooking time: **20 minutes**	**300 ml (½ pint) semi-skimmed milk** **2 tablespoons freshly grated Parmesan cheese**
Oven temperature: **190°C (375°F) Gas Mark 5**	**large pinch of ground nutmeg** **vegetable oil, for oiling** **salt and pepper**
Serves: **6**	

Cut the broccoli into small florets and slice the stems thickly. Put them into a steamer set over boiling water, cover the pan and cook for 3 minutes. Add the spinach and cook for a further 1 minute, or until just wilted.

Beat together the eggs, milk, Parmesan, nutmeg and a little salt and pepper in a jug. Divide the broccoli and spinach between the sections of a lightly oiled, deep 12-section muffin tin, then cover with the egg mixture. Bake in a preheated oven, 190°C (375°F), Gas Mark 5, for about 15 minutes until lightly browned, well risen and the egg mixture has set. Leave in the tin for 1–2 minutes, then loosen the edges with a knife and turn out. Serve 2–3 eggahs per person.

NUTRITIONAL INFORMATION As well as being a rich source of beta-carotene and the carotenoid lutein, which may be important in eye health, spinach is an important source of folate. It is also really versatile and tastes great raw in salads, or in hot dishes, such as omelettes and bakes. The presence of vitamin C-rich broccoli and spinach in this recipe aids the absorption of iron provided by the eggs.

145 kcals (606 kj) ▪ **low fat** ▪ **low carb** ▪ **low GI** ▪ **source of antioxidants** ▪ **source of iron**

60 Red onions stuffed with mushrooms and red rice

Preparation time: **25 minutes**	**4 large red onions, peeled and left whole** **2 tablespoons olive oil** **125 g (4 oz) mushrooms, finely chopped**
Cooking time: **1½ hours**	**75 g (3 oz) red or brown rice** **1 tablespoon chopped parsley** **300 ml (½ pint) water**
Oven temperature: **190°C (375°F) Gas Mark 5**	**1 tablespoon seedless sultanas (optional)** **1 tablespoon freshly grated Parmesan cheese**
Serves: **4**	**salt and pepper**

TO SERVE:
olive oil
coriander leaves

Cut the top off each onion and scoop out the centre with a teaspoon. Finely chop the scooped-out onion. Heat the oil in a large frying pan and gently fry the chopped onion until soft and golden brown. Add the mushrooms and cook for a further 5 minutes, stirring frequently, until they are cooked.

Meanwhile, put the onion cups into a saucepan of boiling water and simmer for 10 minutes, or until they begin to soften. Drain well.

Add the rice, parsley, salt and pepper to taste and measurement water to the mushrooms. Bring to the boil and boil for 5 minutes. Cover the pan and simmer for a further 30 minutes, or until the grains are soft. Add more water if the rice looks dry. Stir the sultanas, if using, into the rice mixture and spoon the mixture into the onions.

Put the onions into a roasting tin, cover with foil and bake in a preheated oven, 190°C (375°F), Gas Mark 5, for 30 minutes. Remove the foil, sprinkle the onions with Parmesan and cook for a further 10 minutes. Serve the onions drizzled with extra oil and topped with coriander.

165 kcals (690 kj) ▪ **low fat** ▪ **low GI** ▪ **high fibre** ▪ **source of antioxidants**

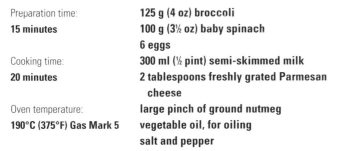

4 Salads

61 Spiced orange and avocado salad

Preparation time:
15 minutes

Serves: **4**

4 large juicy oranges
2 small ripe avocados, stoned and peeled
2 teaspoons cardamom pods
3 tablespoons olive oil
1 tablespoon clear honey
good pinch of ground allspice
2 teaspoons lemon juice
salt and pepper
watercress sprigs, to garnish

Remove the rind and pith from the oranges. Working over a bowl to catch the juice, cut between the membranes to remove the segments.

Slice the avocados and toss gently with the orange segments. Pile on to serving plates.

Reserve a few whole cardamom pods for decoration. Crush the remaining pods in a mortar with a pestle to extract the seeds, or place in a small bowl and crush with the end of a rolling pin. Pick out and discard the pods. Mix the seeds with the oil, honey, allspice, lemon juice, salt and pepper to taste and reserved orange juice.

Garnish the salads with watercress sprigs and serve with the dressing.

NUTRITIONAL INFORMATION Avocados are packed with nutrition – healthy monounsaturated fats, protein, vitamins A and B, calcium and iron, as well as the anti-cholesterol agent beta-sitosterol and the anti-cancer agent glutathione.

312 kcals (1310 kj) ■ **low GI** ■ **source of iron** ■ **source of protein** ■ **source of vitamins A, B, C and E**

62 Orange and almond couscous salad

Preparation time:
15 minutes, plus standing

Cooking time:
5 minutes

Serves: **6**

250 ml (8 fl oz) apple juice
175 g (6 oz) couscous
½ red pepper, cored, deseeded and diced
4 tablespoons chopped parsley
3 tablespoons chopped mint
25 g (1 oz) currants
2 oranges, segmented
1 red onion, sliced
25 g (1 oz) flaked almonds

CITRUS DRESSING:
juice of 1 orange
juice of 1 lemon or lime
2 teaspoons olive or hazelnut oil
1 teaspoon honey

Pour the apple juice into a saucepan and bring to the boil, then slowly stir in the couscous. Remove the pan from heat, cover and leave to stand for 10 minutes. Fluff up the couscous with a fork.

Add the pepper, herbs and currants to the couscous and toss to combine. Transfer the couscous to a serving bowl and scatter with the orange segments and onion.

To make the dressing, put all the ingredients into a small saucepan and heat gently to melt the honey – do not allow it to boil.

Drizzle the dressing over the salad, sprinkle it with almonds and serve.

NUTRITIONAL INFORMATION Almonds contain the amino acid arginine (among other vital nutrients), thought to improve the health of artery linings and reduce the risk of heart disease.

210 kcals (882 kj) ■ **low fat** ■ **source of antioxidants** ■ **source of vitamins C and E**

63 Moroccan tomato and chickpea salad

Preparation time:
10 minutes, plus infusing

Serves: 4

1 red onion, finely sliced
2 x 400 g (13 oz) cans chickpeas, drained and rinsed
4 tomatoes, chopped
4 tablespoons lemon juice
1 tablespoon olive oil
handful of herbs (such as mint and parsley), chopped
pinch of paprika
pinch of ground cumin
salt and pepper

Mix together all the ingredients in a large non-metallic bowl. Set aside for 10 minutes to allow the flavours to infuse, then serve.

298 kcals (1250 kj) ▪ low fat ▪ low GI ▪ high fibre ▪ source of antioxidants

64 Warm aubergine salad

Preparation time:
10 minutes, plus cooling

Cooking time:
10 minutes

Serves: 4

2 tablespoons olive oil
2 aubergines, cut into small cubes
1 red onion, finely sliced
2 tablespoons capers, roughly chopped
4 tomatoes, chopped
4 tablespoons chopped parsley
1 tablespoon balsamic vinegar

Heat the oil in a large nonstick frying pan and fry the aubergines for 10 minutes until golden and softened. Add the onion, capers, tomatoes, parsley and vinegar and stir to combine.

Remove the pan from the heat and allow the salad to cool for about 10 minutes before serving.

NUTRITIONAL INFORMATION The purple colour of aubergine skin is due to a type of anthocyanin, which acts as an antioxidant. The aubergine is also low in calories. However, it does soak up oil, so be careful when cooking it.

113 kcals (473 kj) ▪ low fat ▪ low carb ▪ low GI ▪ source of antioxidants

65 Summer vegetable salad

Preparation time:
10 minutes, plus infusing

Cooking time:
1 minute

Serves: **4**

2 courgettes
2 carrots
150 g (5 oz) mangetout, halved
   lengthways
1 red pepper, cored, deseeded and sliced
150 g (5 oz) bean sprouts
1 red chilli, finely sliced
4 tablespoons chopped coriander leaves
2 tablespoons sesame seeds, toasted
1 tablespoon sesame oil
grated rind and juice of 1 lime

Using a vegetable peeler, slice the courgettes and the carrots into fine ribbons. Put them into a saucepan of boiling water, then immediately drain them and refresh under cold running water.

Toss the courgette and carrot ribbons with the mangetout, pepper, bean sprouts, chilli, coriander, sesame seeds, oil and lime rind and juice and set aside for 20 minutes to allow the flavours to infuse. Serve the salad in a large bowl.

COOK'S NOTES Sesame seeds have a rich, sweet, slightly burnt flavour, which is enhanced by toasting or dry-frying them before use until they jump vigorously in the pan. Black sesame seeds are less common than white ones, but taste the same; the choice of black sesame seeds is therefore more often for the sake of appearance.

134 kcals (563 kj) ▪ **low fat** ▪ **low carb** ▪ **low GI** ▪
source of antioxidants ▪ **source of vitamin C**

66 Glass noodle salad

Preparation time:
15 minutes, plus soaking

Cooking time:
3–4 minutes

Serves: **4**

200 g (7 oz) dried glass noodles, soaked
   and drained
1 tomato, halved and sliced
20 g (¾ oz) celery stick, chopped
20 g (¾ oz) spring onions, chopped
1 onion, halved and sliced
50 g (2 oz) green pepper, cored, deseeded
   and chopped
juice of 2 limes
5 small green chillies, finely chopped
2 teaspoons sugar
25 g (1 oz) crushed roasted peanuts
1 teaspoon crushed dried chillies
½ teaspoon salt
2½ teaspoons Thai fish sauce
coriander sprigs, to garnish

Cook the noodles in a saucepan of boiling water for 3–4 minutes, then drain and rinse under cold running water to prevent further cooking.

Cut the noodles into 12 cm (5 inch) lengths. Return them to the pan and add all the remaining ingredients. Mix thoroughly for 2 minutes.

Serve the salad at room temperature, garnished with coriander sprigs.

COOK'S NOTES To make crushed roasted peanuts, dry-fry the nuts in a frying pan until they turn golden, then allow to cool. Place them in a polythene bag and break into small pieces with a rolling pin.

258 kcals (1078 kj) ▪ **low fat** ▪ **low GI** ▪ **source of**
protein ▪ **source of vitamin C**

Preparation time: 10 minutes	**175 g (6 oz) dried rigatoni** **4 tablespoons low-fat mayonnaise** **juice of ½ lemon**
Cooking time: 10–12 minutes	**6 tomatoes, skinned, deseeded and** **chopped** **125 g (4 oz) green beans, cooked**
Serves: **6**	**12 black olives, pitted** **200 g (7 oz) can tuna in brine, drained and** **flaked** **salt and pepper** **50 g (2 oz) can anchovy fillets, rinsed and** **drained, to garnish** **1 small lettuce, shredded, to serve**

Cook the pasta in a large saucepan of salted water for 10–12 minutes, or according to the packet instructions, until al dente. Drain well. Mix together the mayonnaise and lemon juice and mix a little of this dressing with the pasta. Stir well to combine.

When the pasta is cool, turn it into a bowl and mix with the tomatoes, beans, olives and tuna. Season to taste with salt and pepper.

Toss the salad lightly in the remaining dressing and serve on a bed of shredded lettuce, garnished with anchovies.

Preparation time: 10 minutes	**175 g (6 oz) baby spinach** **125 g (4 oz) button mushrooms, thinly** **sliced**
Serves: **6**	**25 g (1 oz) hazelnuts, chopped**
	YOGURT DRESSING: **2 teaspoons olive oil** **2 tablespoons white wine vinegar** **1 garlic clove, chopped** **2 tablespoons chopped parsley** **3 tablespoons low-fat natural yogurt** **salt and pepper**

To make the dressing, put all the ingredients into a food processor or blender and whiz until smooth.

Tear the spinach leaves into pieces and put them into a salad bowl. Add the sliced mushrooms and hazelnuts and toss together.

Spoon in the dressing and toss again to blend thoroughly. Alternatively, serve the dressing separately.

NUTRITIONAL INFORMATION Tomatoes are a valuable source of beta-carotene, vitamins C and E and potassium, and are particularly rich in lycopene, a potent antioxidant that may protect against cancer of the prostate and breast.

133 kcals (556 kj) ▪ low fat ▪ low carb ▪ low GI ▪
source of antioxidants ▪ source of vitamins C and E

62 kcals (261 kj) ▪ low fat ▪ low carb ▪ low GI ▪
source of iron ▪ source of potassium

69 Bulgar wheat salad with fennel and orange

Preparation time:
10 minutes, plus cooling

Cooking time:
10–12 minutes

Serves: **4**

150 g (5 oz) bulgar wheat
2 tablespoons olive oil
**2 fennel bulbs, trimmed, cored and finely
    sliced**
175 g (6 oz) baby spinach
3 oranges, segmented
2 tablespoons pumpkin seeds, toasted

YOGURT DRESSING:
4 tablespoons low-fat natural yogurt
2 tablespoons chopped coriander leaves
½ small cucumber, finely chopped
salt (optional) and pepper

Prepare the bulgar wheat according to the packet instructions. Set aside to cool. Heat half the oil in a frying pan and fry the fennel for 8–10 minutes until tender and browned. Add the spinach to the pan and stir through until just wilted.

Toss the contents of the pan through the bulgar wheat, then add the orange segments and pumpkin seeds. Mix together all the dressing ingredients with the remaining oil, stir through the salad and serve.

NUTRITIONAL INFORMATION Bulgar wheat is wheat that has been steamed, hulled and cracked. It retains the goodness of the grain, providing vitamins B and E as well as fibre.

324 kcals (1359 kj) ■ low GI ■ high fibre ■ source of iron ■ source of vitamins B, C and E

70 Beetroot, spinach and orange salad

Preparation time:
20 minutes, plus cooling

Cooking time:
1–2 hours

Oven temperature:
200°C (400°F) Gas Mark 6

Serves: **4**

500 g (1 lb) raw whole beetroots
2 garlic cloves
handful of oregano leaves
1 teaspoon olive oil
1 tablespoon balsamic vinegar
200 g (7 oz) baby spinach
2 oranges, segmented
pepper
chopped oregano, to garnish

OLIVE VINAIGRETTE:
2 tablespoons balsamic vinegar
2 tablespoons lime juice
1 garlic clove
**1–2 black olives, pitted and finely
    chopped**
1 teaspoon Dijon mustard

To bake the beetroot, put each beetroot on a piece of foil large enough to enclose it loosely with the garlic cloves and oregano leaves. Season to taste with pepper and drizzle with the oil and vinegar. Gather up the foil loosely and fold over at the top to seal. Put on a baking sheet and bake in a preheated oven, 200°C (400°F), Gas Mark 6, for 1–2 hours, depending on size of the beetroot, until tender.

Remove the beetroot from the oven and allow them to cool, then peel and slice. Discard the garlic.

To make the vinaigrette, put all the ingredients into a screw-top jar, replace the lid and shake well.

Arrange a layer of spinach in a large salad bowl, followed by alternate layers of beetroot and orange. Drizzle over the dressing and season to taste with pepper. Garnish with chopped oregano.

115 kcals (484 kj) ■ low fat ■ low GI ■ source of antioxidants ■ source of iron ■ source of vitamin C

71 Watercress and pine nut salad

72 Feta salad

Preparation time:
15 minutes

Cooking time:
2 minutes

Serves: **4**

1 firm ripe mango
1 pink grapefruit
125 g (4 oz) watercress
75 g (3 oz) pine nuts
salt and pepper

SWEET MUSTARD DRESSING:
3 tablespoons olive oil
1 tablespoon white wine vinegar
1 teaspoon Dijon mustard
1 teaspoon soft light brown sugar

To make the dressing, mix together all the ingredients and season to taste with salt and pepper.

Slice the mango lengthways either side of the thin central stone. Remove the skin and discard, then slice or dice the flesh. Remove the rind and pith from the grapefruit. Working over a bowl to catch the juice, cut between the membranes to remove the segments.

Squeeze the remaining juice from the grapefruit membrane and whisk 1 tablespoon of it into the dressing. Put the watercress into a bowl with the mango pieces and grapefruit segments.

Heat a dry frying pan until hot, add the pine nuts and toast lightly, shaking the pan frequently. Remove the pine nuts from the heat and scatter them over the salad with a spoon. Drizzle the dressing over the salad and serve immediately.

NUTRITIONAL INFORMATION Watercress is a good source of the antioxidant vitamins A, C and E. It also contains phenethyl isothio-cyanate (gluconasturtin), which combats the carcinogen NNK – if eaten in large quantities, this can protect against lung cancer.

289 kcals (1213 kj) ■ low carb ■ low GI ■ source of antioxidants ■ source of protein ■ source of vitamin C

Preparation time:
10 minutes

Cooking time:
3 minutes

Serves: **1**

1 Little Gem lettuce
25 g (1 oz) cucumber, chopped
2 tomatoes, chopped
¼ red onion, sliced
25 g (1 oz) vegetarian feta cheese, crumbled
2 mini pitta breads
1 tablespoon Low-Calorie French Dressing (see recipe 78)

Tear the lettuce into small pieces. In a large bowl, mix together the lettuce, cucumber, tomatoes, onion and feta.

Toast the pitta breads.

Transfer the salad to a plate, drizzle over the dressing and serve with the pitta breads.

300 kcals (1273 kj) ■ low fat ■ source of antioxidants ■ source of calcium

73 Moroccan griddled vegetable salad

Preparation time:
15 minutes

Cooking time:
45–50 minutes

Serves: **4**

2 aubergines, sliced lengthways
1 onion, sliced
4 garlic cloves, sliced
1 red pepper, cored, deseeded and
  quartered
1 orange pepper, cored, deseeded and
  quartered
4 tomatoes, halved
1 red chilli, halved and deseeded, plus
  2 whole red chillies to garnish
  (optional)
½ teaspoon caraway seeds
½ teaspoon ground cumin
50 g (2 oz) pitted black olives
1 bunch of coriander, roughly chopped
2 tablespoons olive oil
salt and pepper

Heat a griddle pan. Put the aubergine slices on the griddle and cook for 5 minutes on each side. Transfer to a mixing bowl.

Griddle the onion slices for 5 minutes on each side and add to the aubergine in the bowl. Griddle the garlic slices for 2 minutes on each side and add to the bowl. Griddle the pepper quarters for 5 minutes on each side, then the tomato halves for 5 minutes on the skin side and add to the bowl. Finally, griddle the chilli halves for 5 minutes on one side and the whole chillies on each side, if using. Finely chop the chilli halves and add them to the bowl.

Crush the caraway seeds in a mortar with a pestle. Add to the griddled vegetables with the cumin, olives, coriander, oil and salt and pepper to taste. Garnish with the griddled red chillies, if using. Serve the salad at room temperature.

165 kcals (690 kj) ■ **low carb** ■ **low GI** ■ **source of antioxidants** ■ **source of vitamins A, C and E**

74 Herb and asparagus salad

Preparation time:
10 minutes

Cooking time:
about 5 minutes

Serves: **8**

1 garlic clove, halved
1 Cos lettuce, roughly torn
125 g (4 oz) lamb's lettuce
1 bunch of watercress
1 punnet of mustard and cress
1 bunch of rocket
1 small bunch of chervil
1 bunch of chives
1 bunch of flat leaf parsley
1 bunch of basil
1 bunch of mint
1 avocado, peeled, stoned and chopped
175 g (6 oz) young asparagus

DRESSING:
2 tablespoons olive oil
1 tablespoon white wine vinegar
2 garlic cloves, crushed
¼ teaspoon soft brown sugar
¼ teaspoon sweet paprika

Rub around the inside of a large salad bowl with the cut garlic clove, then discard. Next, wash and prepare the salad greens.

Chop the chives and parsley and strip the leaves from the basil and mint, discarding the stems. Place the salad greens and herbs in the salad bowl with the chopped avocado and mix well.

Heat a griddle pan, add the asparagus in a single layer and cook for 5 minutes, turning constantly, until charred and beginning to soften.

To make the dressing, place all the ingredients in a screw-top jar and shake well. Just before serving put the hot asparagus on the top of the salad, pour the dressing on top and toss well.

78 kcals (323 kj) ■ **low fat** ■ **low carb** ■ **low GI** ■ **source of vitamins A, B and E**

75 Couscous and griddled vegetable salad

76 Griddled greens

Preparation time:
15 minutes, plus standing and cooling

Cooking time:
40 minutes

Serves: **4**

1 aubergine, sliced
2 garlic cloves, sliced
2 green chillies
1 red pepper
2 red onions
1 courgette, sliced
125 g (4 oz) couscous
½ teaspoon cumin
½ teaspoon paprika
pinch of dried chilli flakes
5 tablespoons olive oil
salt and pepper
1 bunch of coriander, chopped, to garnish

Heat a griddle pan. Put the aubergine slices on the griddle and cook for 5 minutes on each side. Remove to a large bowl. Griddle the garlic slices for 1 minute on each side, then add to the aubergine.

Griddle the chillies for 5 minutes together with the pepper for 10 minutes until charred all over. Set aside. Cut the onions into wedges, keeping the root ends intact to hold the wedges together. Griddle for 5 minutes on each side, then add to the aubergine. Griddle the courgette slices for 4 minutes on each side and add to the bowl.

Tip the couscous into a large heatproof bowl and add enough boiling water to cover. Cover and leave to stand for 10 minutes. Fluff up the couscous with a fork.

When the chillies and pepper are cool enough, remove the skin and discard, then deseed and chop the flesh. Roughly chop all the griddled vegetables and add to the couscous. Add the cumin, paprika, chilli flakes and salt and pepper to taste and mix well. Drizzle with the oil and garnish with the chopped coriander.

Preparation time:
10 minutes

Cooking time:
about 20 minutes

Serves: **4**

2 courgettes, cut into batons
250 g (8 oz) asparagus, trimmed
250 g (8 oz) baby leeks, trimmed
2 red peppers, cored, deseeded and quartered
4 tablespoons olive oil
2 tablespoons balsamic vinegar
salt and pepper
basil leaves, to garnish

Heat a griddle pan. Put the courgettes on the griddle and cook for 6 minutes, turning occasionally. Transfer to a bowl.

Griddle the asparagus and leeks for 5 minutes, turning them occasionally, and add to the courgettes.

Finally, griddle the pepper quarters on the skin side only for 5 minutes and add to the bowl. Mix the vegetables together. Add the oil, vinegar and salt and pepper to taste and toss well. Garnish with basil leaves and serve.

262 kcals (1095 kj) ■ **low carb** ■ **low GI** ■ **source of antioxidants**

208 kcals (869 kj) ■ **low carb** ■ **low GI** ■ **source of antioxidants** ■ **source of vitamin A**

Preparation time:
5 minutes

Cooking time:
5 minutes

Serves: 2

250 g (8 oz) okra, thinly sliced
2 large garlic cloves, crushed
150–175 ml (5–6 fl oz) water
175 g (6 oz) canned butter beans, drained
  and rinsed
175 g (6 oz) canned red kidney beans,
  drained and rinsed
2 teaspoons lemon juice
2 teaspoons olive oil
large handful of mixed herbs, chopped
pepper
2 thick slices of crusty wholemeal bread,
  to serve

Preparation time:
10 minutes, plus
marinating

Cooking time:
5 minutes

Serves: 8

1 kg (2 lb) frozen whole green beans
500 g (1 lb) button mushrooms
juice of ½ lemon
salt

LOW-CALORIE FRENCH DRESSING:
6 tablespoons olive oil
2 tablespoons wine vinegar
½ teaspoon mustard
¼ tablespoon sugar
½ small onion, grated
a little ground coriander
3 tablespoons chopped parsley
salt and pepper

Put the okra, garlic cloves and measurement water into a saucepan, cover the pan and bring to the boil. Reduce the heat and simmer gently for 3–4 minutes until soft. Drain.

Meanwhile, in a separate saucepan, gently heat the butter beans and kidney beans with the lemon juice. Strain, then add the okra, garlic, oil, herbs and pepper to taste. Stir gently, then serve with thick slices of wholemeal bread.

Cook the beans in a saucepan of lightly salted boiling water until just tender, then cool under cold running water. Drain thoroughly.

Finely slice the mushrooms and sprinkle with lemon juice. To make the dressing, put all the ingredients into a bowl and whisk until thickened. Pour it over the mushrooms. Cover and leave to marinate for 1–2 hours, turning gently from time to time.

Toss the mushroom mixture carefully with the green beans and serve in a large serving dish or on individual plates.

NUTRITIONAL INFORMATION This is a very high-fibre recipe and therefore very filling and satisfying. Beans, of course, are a good source of fibre, but okra is fibre-rich too. Be careful to drink plenty of water when fibre intake is increased, as fibre absorbs fluid and swells.

325 kcals (1365 kj) ■ **low fat** ■ **low GI** ■ **high fibre** ■ **source of protein**

173 kcals (726 kj) ■ **low carb** ■ **low GI** ■ **source of potassium**

79 Warm salad of turkey, red pepper and lemon

80 Duck and green papaya salad

Preparation time:
10 minutes

Cooking time:
12 minutes

Serves: **4**

2 Little Gem lettuces, leaves separated
1 tablespoon olive oil
1 red pepper, cored, deseeded and cut lengthways into thin strips
500 g (1 lb) cooked turkey, cut diagonally into thin strips
lemon wedges, to garnish

DRESSING:
1½ tablespoons olive oil
2 tablespoons lemon juice
1 garlic clove, crushed
1 teaspoon Dijon mustard
salt and pepper

Preparation time:
10 minutes, plus marinating and cooling

Cooking time:
1 hour

Oven temperature.
150°C (300°F) Gas Mark 2

Serves: **4**

2 duck breast fillets, skin and fat removed
1 garlic clove, finely chopped
1 dessertspoon golden caster sugar
75 ml (3 fl oz) white rice vinegar
1 small red chilli, finely chopped
salt
1 green papaya, shredded

MARINADE:
2 teaspoons clear honey
1 shallot, finely chopped
2 garlic cloves, finely chopped
1 lemon grass stalk, finely chopped
pinch of Chinese five-spice powder
pinch of ground cinnamon
1 small red chilli, finely chopped
salt and pepper

TO GARNISH:
coriander leaves
peanuts

To make the dressing, put all the ingredients into a bowl and whisk until thickened. Tear the lettuce leaves roughly and put them into a large salad bowl.

Heat the oil in a heavy-based frying pan and fry the pepper strips, stirring frequently, for 5 minutes. Add the turkey strips and cook, stirring, for 5 minutes until tender and heated through.

Remove the turkey and pepper strips from the pan with a slotted spoon and arrange on top of the lettuce.

Pour the dressing into the pan, increase the heat to high and stir until sizzling. Pour the dressing over the salad and toss. Serve at once, garnished with lemon wedges.

Mix together all the marinade ingredients in a bowl. Add the duck fillets, cover and leave to marinate for 2–3 hours.

Put the duck fillets and the marinade into a roasting tin and roast in a preheated oven, 150°C (300°F), Gas Mark 2, for 1 hour. Remove the fillets and allow to cool, then cut them into slices.

Combine the garlic, sugar, vinegar, chilli and salt to taste in a large bowl, stir in the papaya shreds, then add the sliced duck. Serve the salad sprinkled with coriander leaves and peanuts to garnish.

NUTRITIONAL INFORMATION Dark turkey meat contains almost twice the amount of fat as lighter turkey meat, so choose the lighter meat for a lower-fat option.

232 kcals (970 kj) ■ **low carb** ■ **low GI** ■ **source of antioxidants**

123 kcals (514 kj) ■ **low fat** ■ **low carb** ■ **source of vitamin C**

81 Cajun potato, prawn and avocado salad

Preparation time:
10 minutes

Cooking time:
15–20 minutes

Serves: 2

300 g (10 oz) baby new potatoes, halved
1 tablespoon olive oil
250 g (8 oz) cooked peeled king prawns
I garlic clove, crushed
4 spring onions, finely sliced
2 teaspoons Cajun seasoning
1 ripe avocado, stoned, peeled and diced
handful of alfalfa sprouts
salt

Cook the potatoes in a large saucepan of lightly salted boiling water for 10–15 minutes, or until tender. Drain well.

Heat the oil in a large nonstick frying pan and stir-fry the prawns, garlic, spring onions and Cajun seasoning for 2–3 minutes, or until the prawns are hot. Stir in the potatoes and cook for a further 1 minute. Transfer to a serving dish.

Stir in the avocado, top with the alfalfa sprouts and serve.

82 Pomelo and prawn salad

Preparation time:
10 minutes

Cooking time:
1–2 minutes

Serves: 4

1 large pomelo or grapefruit
40 g (1½ oz) peanuts, toasted and roughly chopped
175 g (6 oz) raw king prawns, peeled and deveined
2 tablespoons grapefruit juice
½ tablespoon Thai fish sauce
4 spring onions, finely shredded
6 mint leaves, finely shredded
1 large red chilli, finely sliced
pepper
pinch of grated nutmeg
4–5 salad leaves

Cut the pomelo or grapefruit in half and scoop out the segments and juice. Discard the pith and thick membrane surrounding each segment, then break the flesh into small pieces. Mix the toasted peanuts with the pomelo or grapefruit.

Simmer the prawns in a saucepan of boiling water for 1–2 minutes, or until pink and cooked through. Drain well and add to the pomelo or grapefruit with the grapefruit juice, fish sauce, spring onions and mint.

Sprinkle the chilli, pepper and nutmeg over the salad and toss well. Line a bowl with the salad leaves and spoon in the salad. Serve the salad immediately.

NUTRITIONAL INFORMATION Prawns and other shellfish are a low-fat, low-calorie source of protein and many minerals, including selenium, zinc and magnesium, as well as the B-group vitamins.

451 kcals (1885 kj) ▪ low carb ▪ low GI ▪ high fibre ▪ source of protein ▪ source of vitamins B and E

145 kcals (606 kj) ▪ low fat ▪ low carb ▪ low GI ▪ high fibre ▪ source of protein ▪ source of vitamin C

83 Lentil salad with parma ham crisps

84 Parma ham and vegetable salad

Preparation time: **10 minutes**	**2 tablespoons olive oil**
	1 garlic clove, crushed
	4 spring onions, sliced
Cooking time: **5 minutes**	**2 x 400 g (13 oz) cans green lentils, rinsed and drained**
	2 tablespoons balsamic vinegar
Serves: **4**	**3 tablespoons chopped herbs (such as parsley, oregano or basil)**
	125 g (4 oz) cherry tomatoes, halved
	85 g (3¼ oz) sliced Parma ham

Heat the oil in a nonstick saucepan and fry the garlic and spring onions for 2 minutes. Stir in the lentils, vinegar, herbs and tomatoes, then set aside.

Heat a frying pan until hot and dry-fry the Parma ham for 1–2 minutes, or until crisp. Arrange the lentil salad on a large serving dish, place the Parma ham on top and serve.

Preparation time: **10 minutes**	**2 red onions**
	2 red peppers, cored, deseeded and cut into flat pieces
Cooking time: **40–45 minutes**	**2 courgettes, cut into lengths**
	1 aubergine, cut into lengths
	1 bunch of asparagus, trimmed
Serves: **4**	**8 slices of Parma ham**
	1 bunch of basil, roughly chopped
	4 tablespoons olive oil
	2 tablespoons balsamic vinegar
	salt and pepper
	basil sprig, to garnish

Heat a griddle pan. Cut the onions into wedges, keeping the root ends intact to hold the wedges together. Griddle all the vegetables as follows, then put them into a large serving bowl: onions for 5 minutes on each side; peppers for 5 minutes on the skin side only; courgettes for 3 minutes on each side; aubergines for 4 minutes on each side; asparagus for 4 minutes on one side only. Toss all the griddled vegetables together well.

Griddle the slices of Parma ham for 4 minutes on each side, or until they become crisp.

Add the chopped basil to the vegetables with the oil, vinegar and a little salt and pepper. Top the vegetables with the Parma ham and serve immediately, garnished with a basil sprig.

NUTRITIONAL INFORMATION Lentils are rich in soluble fibre, folate and iron. Vitamin C increases the absorption of iron, so the combination here of lentils with cherry tomatoes has an added benefit.

238 kcals (1001 kj) ■ low fat ■ low GI ■ source of antioxidants ■ source of iron ■ source of protein

294 kcals (1229 kj) ■ low carb ■ low GI ■ source of antioxidants ■ source of vitamin A

85 Griddled summer chicken salad

Preparation time:
15 minutes

Cooking time:
45 minutes

Serves: **4**

4 skinless chicken fillets, about 125 g (4 oz) each
2 small red onions
2 red peppers, cored, deseeded and cut into flat pieces
1 bunch of asparagus, trimmed
200 g (7 oz) new potatoes, boiled and halved
1 bunch of basil
5 tablespoons olive oil
2 tablespoons balsamic vinegar
salt and pepper

Heat a griddle pan. Put the chicken fillets on the griddle and cook for 10 minutes on each side. Remove them from the griddle and cut roughly into chunks.

Cut the onions into wedges, keeping the root ends intact to hold the wedges together. Put on the griddle and cook for 5 minutes on each side. Remove and set aside.

Put the pepper pieces on the griddle and cook for 8 minutes on the skin side only, so that the skins are charred and blistered. Remove and set aside, then cook the asparagus on the griddle for 6 minutes, turning frequently. When the peppers are cool enough to handle, remove the skins and discard.

Put the potatoes into a large bowl. Tear the basil, reserving a few leaves for garnish, and add to the bowl with the griddled chicken and the vegetables. Add the oil, vinegar and salt and pepper to taste. Toss the salad and serve garnished with the reserved basil leaves.

908 kcals (3795 kj) ■ **low carb** ■ **low GI** ■ **source of antioxidants** ■ **source of protein** ■ **source of vitamin C**

86 Smoked chicken salad

Preparation time:
10 minutes

Cooking time:
5 minutes

Serves: **2**

150 g (5 oz) asparagus, trimmed and cut into 5 cm (2 inch) lengths
200 g (7 oz) smoked chicken breast, cut into bite-sized pieces
125 g (4 oz) cherry tomatoes, halved
300 g (10 oz) canned cannellini beans, drained and rinsed
handful of chives, snipped

DRESSING:
2 tablespoons olive oil
1 garlic clove, crushed
2 teaspoons clear honey
2 teaspoons balsamic vinegar
2 teaspoons wholegrain mustard

Cook the asparagus in a large saucepan of lightly salted boiling water for about 4 minutes, or until just tender. Drain and plunge into cold water to prevent it cooking further. Pat dry with kitchen paper.

Put the chicken into a large bowl, add the tomatoes, beans, asparagus and chives and mix well.

To make the dressing, whisk all the ingredients together in a small bowl. Pour the dressing over the salad and toss well to coat. Serve the salad immediately.

NUTRITIONAL INFORMATION Like all beans and pulses, cannellini beans pack a nutritional punch. Aside from their high protein content, trace minerals and B vitamins, they are a good source of insoluble fibre, which is important for good bowel health.

474 kcals (1981 kj) ■ **low GI** ■ **high fibre** ■ **source of antioxidants** ■ **source of protein**

87 Pearl barley salad with griddled chicken

88 Mango, avocado and smoked chicken salad

Preparation time:
10 minutes

Cooking time:
10 minutes

Serves: **4**

4 boneless, skinless chicken breasts
1 tablespoon olive oil
125 g (4 oz) pearl barley, cooked
  according to the packet instructions
1 red onion, finely chopped
1 red chilli, finely chopped
4 tablespoons chopped coriander leaves
grated rind and juice of 2 limes
1 red pepper, cored, deseeded and finely
  chopped
salt and pepper

TO GARNISH:
flat leaf parsley sprigs
lime wedges

Brush each chicken breast with a little of the oil. Heat a griddle pan. Put the chicken on the griddle and cook for 4–5 minutes on each side until browned and cooked through. Cut each breast into 4 slices.

Stir the remaining oil into the barley, then add the onion, chilli, coriander, lime rind and juice and pepper. Season to taste with salt and pepper and stir to combine.

Serve the barley topped with the chicken, garnished with parsley sprigs and lime wedges.

Preparation time:
15 minutes

Serves: **4**

2 ripe avocados
2 tablespoons lemon juice
1 small mango
3 tablespoons olive oil
1 teaspoon wholegrain mustard
1 teaspoon clear honey
2 teaspoons cider vinegar
handful of watercress
50 g (2 oz) cooked beetroot, finely sliced
175 g (6 oz) smoked chicken breast,
  thinly sliced
salt and pepper

Halve, stone and peel the avocados. Slice or dice the avocado flesh and put into a shallow bowl with the lemon juice.

Slice the mango lengthways either side of the thin central stone. Remove the skin and discard, then slice or dice the flesh.

Mix together the oil, mustard, honey, vinegar and salt and pepper to taste in a small bowl. Remove the avocado from the lemon juice and stir the juice into the dressing.

Arrange the watercress and beetroot on 4 plates or in a salad bowl and add the avocado and mango. Drizzle the dressing over the salad and top with the slices of smoked chicken. Serve immediately.

NUTRITIONAL INFORMATION Pearl barley is high in soluble fibre and can be used as a substitute for rice.

327 kcals (1367 kj) ▪ **low fat** ▪ **low GI** ▪ **high fibre** ▪ **source of antioxidants**

254 kcals (1062 kj) ▪ **low carb** ▪ **low GI** ▪ **source of antioxidants** ▪ **source of vitamins C and E**

5 Fish and Shellfish

89 Monkfish brochettes with cannellini beans

90 Stuffed monkfish with balsamic dressing

Preparation time: **10 minutes**	**250 g (8 oz) monkfish, cut into 6 pieces** **6 slices of Parma ham** **6 cherry tomatoes**
Cooking time: **6–8 minutes**	**1 yellow pepper, cored, deseeded and** **cut into 6 pieces** **1 tablespoon olive oil**
Serves: **2**	**300 g (10 oz) canned cannellini beans,** **drained and rinsed** **2 tablespoons ready-made fresh pesto**

Preparation time: **15 minutes**	**125 ml (4 fl oz) balsamic vinegar** **4 monkfish fillets, about 150 g (5 oz) each** **4 teaspoons tapenade**
Cooking time: **20–25 minutes**	**8 basil leaves** **8 rindless rashers of streaky bacon,** **stretched with the back of a knife**
Serves: **4**	**375 g (12 oz) green beans** **125 g (4 oz) frozen peas** **6 spring onions, finely sliced** **125 g (4 oz) feta cheese, crumbled** **2 tablespoons basil oil** **salt**

Wrap each piece of monkfish in a slice of Parma ham. Thread the pieces on to 2 skewers, alternating them with the tomatoes and pepper pieces. Brush the brochettes with the oil and cook under a preheated hot grill for 3–4 minutes. Turn and cook for a further 3 minutes until cooked through.

Meanwhile, put the beans into a nonstick saucepan and cook, stirring, over a low heat for 4–5 minutes, or until hot. Stir in the pesto. Spoon on to 2 plates, top with the brochettes and serve immediately.

Pour the vinegar into a small saucepan. Bring to the boil over a medium heat, then simmer for about 8–10 minutes until it is thick and glossy. Set aside to cool slightly, but keep warm.

Put the monkfish fillets on a chopping board and make a deep incision about 5 cm (2 inches) long in the side of each fillet. Stuff with 1 teaspoon of tapenade and 2 basil leaves. Wrap 2 rashers of bacon around each fillet, sealing in the filling. Fasten with a cocktail stick.

Boil the beans in a saucepan of lightly salted boiling water for 3 minutes. Add the peas and cook for a further 1 minute. Drain and keep warm.

Heat a griddle pan over a medium heat. Put the monkfish on the griddle and cook for 4–5 minutes on each side until cooked through. Set aside and allow to rest for 1–2 minutes.

Meanwhile, toss the beans and peas with the spring onions, feta and basil oil and arrange on warmed serving plates. Top the vegetables with a monkfish fillet and serve immediately, drizzled with the warm balsamic dressing.

NUTRITIONAL INFORMATION Monkfish has a mild, sweet flavour, similar to that of lobster, but its firm and meaty texture makes it ideal for roasting. It may also be used as a meat substitute by those wishing to decrease their saturated fat intake.

575 kcals (2415 kj) ■ **low GI** ■ **high fibre** ■ **source of antioxidants** ■ **source of protein**

422 kcals (1764 kj) ■ **low carb** ■ **source of calcium**

91 Oriental monkfish

Preparation time.
20 minutes

Cooking time:
8–10 minutes

Serves: 4

800 g (1 lb 10 oz) trimmed monkfish fillets
200 g (7 oz) pak choi
2 lemon grass stalks, griddled, to garnish
(optional)
steamed basmati rice, to serve (optional)

ORIENTAL DRESSING:
3 cm (1¼ inch) piece of fresh root ginger,
peeled and finely chopped
3 cm (1¼ inch) piece of galangal, peeled
and finely chopped
2 garlic cloves, chopped
2 kaffir lime leaves, cut into very thin
strips
1 lemon grass stalk, finely sliced
2 red chillies, chopped
4 tablespoons lime juice
2 tablespoons soy sauce

Heat a griddle pan. Pat the monkfish dry with kitchen paper, put on the griddle and cook for 8–10 minutes on each side.

Meanwhile, to make the dressing, mix together all the ingredients in a bowl.

Cut the pak choi in half or into wedges and put them into a steamer over boiling water. Steam for 3 minutes.

When the monkfish is cooked, remove it from the griddle, place on a chopping board and slice into rounds. Toss the monkfish and pak choi with the oriental dressing and serve garnished with the griddled lemon grass stalks, if using, and accompanied by steamed basmati rice, if liked.

198 kcals (828 kj) low fat low carb low GI
source of antioxidants

92 Sardines with citrus mint tabbouleh

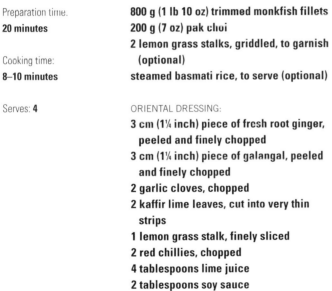

Preparation time:
10 minutes

Cooking time:
10–15 minutes

Serves: 2

4 medium fresh sardines, about 50 g (2 oz)
each, cleaned
oil or lemon juice, for brushing (optional)
flat leaf parsley, to garnish
lemon wedges, to serve

TABBOULEH:
300–350 ml (10–12 fl oz) Chicken Stock
(see Introduction)
50–75 g (2–3 oz) bulgar wheat
1 teaspoon olive oil
grated rind and juice of 1 lemon
handful of mint, roughly chopped

To make the tabbouleh, bring the stock to the boil in a saucepan, add the bulgar wheat and simmer for 10–15 minutes, or until just cooked. Drain well, then stir in the oil, lemon rind and juice and mint. Add a little more stock if the tabbouleh seems too dry.

Meanwhile, cook the sardines under a moderately hot grill, turning them over when they are sizzling. Brush with a very little oil or lemon juice, if liked, but normally they contain sufficient oil.

Arrange the tabbouleh on warmed plates, top with the sardines and sprinkle with the parsley. Serve the lemon wedges on the side.

NUTRITIONAL INFORMATION Sardines are commonly eaten whole in Spain and Portugal, and these, as well as other oily fish, are an integral part of the heart-healthy Mediterranean diet.

327 kcals (1371 kj) low fat low GI source of
omega-3 fatty acids

93 Salmon and asparagus wholewheat spaghetti

94 Crushed new potatoes with herby salmon

Preparation time:
5 minutes

Cooking time:
10–12 minutes

Serves: **2**

125–175 g (4–6 oz) dried wholewheat spaghetti
150 g (5 oz) asparagus tips
125 g (4 oz) smoked salmon, cut into pieces
4 heaped tablespoons low-fat fromage frais
2 tablespoons chopped tarragon
grated nutmeg

Preparation time:
10 minutes

Cooking time:
20 minutes

Serves: **4**

750 g (1½ lb) new potatoes
knob of butter
grated rind and juice of 2 limes
1 bunch of spring onions, sliced
4 pieces of boneless, skinless salmon fillet, about 125 g (4 oz) each
4 tablespoons low-fat crème fraîche
3 tablespoons chopped mixed herbs (such as parsley and dill)
salt and pepper
lime wedges, to garnish

Cook the pasta in a large saucepan of boiling water for 10–12 minutes, or according to the packet instructions, until al dente. Drain and return to the pan.

Meanwhile, cook the asparagus tips in a saucepan of boiling water for 2 minutes, or until just tender. Drain.

Mix the smoked salmon, fromage frais, asparagus, tarragon and a little grated nutmeg into the pasta and serve immediately.

Cook the potatoes in a saucepan of lightly salted boiling water until tender. Drain and lightly crush with a fork.

Stir in the butter, half the lime rind and juice and half the spring onions and season with plenty of pepper.

Put the pieces of salmon on a foil-lined grill pan and cook under a preheated moderate grill for 6–7 minutes, or until the salmon is just cooked, turning them over halfway through cooking.

Mix together the remaining lime rind and juice, spring onions, crème fraîche and herbs. Serve the salmon with the potatoes and the herby sauce, garnished with lime wedges.

NUTRITIONAL INFORMATION New potatoes have a low GI value, so use these instead of boiled, mashed or roasted varieties where possible. They are delicious served with a little butter and chopped mint.

432 kcals (1814 kj) ■ **low fat** ■ **low GI** ■ **high fibre** ■ **source of omega-3 fatty acids** ■ **source of vitamin C**

426 kcals (1790 kj) ■ **low GI** ■ **high fibre** ■ **source of omega-3 fatty acids** ■ **source of protein**

95 Puy lentils with flaked salmon and dill

96 Smoked salmon and cream cheese risotto

Preparation time:
20 minutes, plus cooling and chilling

Cooking time:
40–50 minutes

Oven temperature:
200°C (400°F) Gas Mark 6

Serves: 4

500 g (1 lb) salmon tail fillet
2 tablespoons dry white wine
4 red peppers, halved, cored and deseeded
175 g (6 oz) Puy lentils, well rinsed
large handful of dill, chopped
1 bunch of spring onions, finely sliced
pepper

DRESSING:
2 garlic cloves
handful of flat leaf parsley, chopped
large handful of dill, chopped
1 teaspoon Dijon mustard
2 green chillies, deseeded and chopped
juice of 2 large lemons
1 tablespoon olive oil

Put the salmon on a sheet of foil and spoon over the wine. Gather up the foil and fold it over at the top to seal. Put on a baking sheet and bake in a preheated oven, 200°C (400°F), Gas Mark 6, for 15–20 minutes until cooked. Allow to cool, then flake, cover and chill.

Grill the pepper halves skin side up under a preheated hot grill until charred. Enclose in a polythene bag for a few minutes, then remove and discard the skin and cut the flesh into 2.5 cm (1 inch) cubes.

Whiz together all the dressing ingredients, except the oil, in a food processor or blender until smooth, at the same time drizzling in the oil.

Bring the lentils to the boil in a large saucepan of water, then simmer for 15–20 minutes until cooked but still firm to the bite. Drain and place in a bowl with the peppers, dill, spring onions and pepper to taste. Stir in the dressing. Top the lentils with the salmon, mix gently and serve.

Preparation time:
10 minutes

Cooking time:
about 25 minutes

Serves: 4

2 teaspoons olive oil
1 onion, finely chopped
2 garlic cloves, crushed
300 g (10 oz) arborio rice
150 ml (¼ pint) dry white wine
900 ml (1½ pints) Vegetable Stock (see Introduction), simmering
125 g (4 oz) low-fat cream cheese
125 g (4 oz) smoked salmon, chopped
4 tablespoons chopped herbs (such as chives, parsley or dill)
salt and pepper

Heat the oil in a large saucepan and fry the onion and garlic for 2–3 minutes until they begin to soften.

Add the rice and cook, stirring, for 1 minute. Add the wine and cook, stirring, until it has been absorbed.

Add the stock, a ladleful at a time, stirring constantly, allowing each ladleful to be absorbed before adding the next. Continue until all the stock has been absorbed and the rice is creamy but still firm to the bite. This will take about 20 minutes.

Stir in the cream cheese, smoked salmon and herbs, season to taste with salt and pepper and serve.

NUTRITIONAL INFORMATION Salmon is an oily fish, providing a rich source of omega-3 fatty acids, which will have a beneficial effect on reducing blood clotting and an irregular heartbeat. Canned salmon is also a good source of omega-3 fatty acids, but has a higher salt content than fresh salmon. Try to eat oily fish at least once a week.

466 kcals (1958 kj) ▪ low GI ▪ high fibre ▪ source of iron ▪ source of omega-3 fatty acids ▪ source of protein

438 kcals (1839 kj) ▪ low fat ▪ source of calcium ▪ source of omega-3 fatty acids

97 Poached salmon with hot basil sauce

Preparation time:
20 minutes

Cooking time:
25 minutes

Serves: **4**

**1 large bunch of fresh basil, plus extra
   sprigs to garnish
2 celery sticks, chopped
1 carrot, chopped
1 small courgette, chopped
1 small onion, chopped
4 salmon steaks, about 125 g (4 oz) each
75 ml (3 fl oz) white wine
125 ml (4 fl oz) water
1 teaspoon lemon juice
15 g (½ oz) unsalted butter
salt and pepper
lemon wedges, to garnish
cooked whole green beans, to serve**

Strip the leaves off half the basil and set aside.

Spread the chopped celery, carrot, courgette and onion evenly over the base of a large flameproof dish or pan with a lid, put the salmon steaks on top and cover them with the remaining basil sprigs.

Pour over the wine and measurement water and season to taste with salt and pepper. Bring to the boil, then reduce the heat, cover the pan and simmer for about 10 minutes. Transfer the salmon to a warmed serving dish and keep warm.

Return the poaching liquid and vegetables to the boil and simmer for 5 minutes. Strain into a food processor or blender and add the cooked and uncooked basil. Whiz to a purée and transfer to a saucepan. Bring the purée to the boil and boil until reduced by half.

Remove the pan from the heat, add the lemon juice and stir in the butter. Pour the sauce over the salmon steaks, garnish with lemon wedges and basil sprigs and serve with whole green beans.

289 kcals (1212 kj) ■ low carb ■ low GI ■ source of omega-3 fatty acids

98 Baked trout parcels with tartare sauce

Preparation time:
5–10 minutes

Cooking time:
12–15 minutes

Oven temperature:
200°C (400°F) Gas Mark 6

Serves: **1**

**1 rainbow trout fillet, about 150 g (5 oz)
grated rind and juice of 1 lime
cooked vegetables and potatoes, to serve**

TARTARE SAUCE:
**2 cocktail gherkins, finely chopped
1 teaspoon capers, roughly chopped
2 teaspoons low-fat crème fraîche
1 spring onion, sliced
1 tablespoon chopped parsley**

Put the trout fillet on a piece of foil and sprinkle with half the lime rind and juice. Gather up the foil and fold it over at the top to seal. Put on a baking sheet and bake in a preheated oven, 200°C (400°F), Gas Mark 6, for 12–15 minutes until cooked.

Meanwhile, to make the tartare sauce, combine all the ingredients in a small bowl and stir in the remaining lime rind and juice.

Remove the foil and serve the trout with the tartare sauce and accompanied by potatoes and vegetables.

NUTRITIONAL INFORMATION Trout is a fatty fish, and is therefore a good source of the important omega-3 fish oils that are protective of the heart.

222 kcals (930 kj) ■ low fat ■ low carb ■ low GI ■ source of omega-3 fatty acids

99 Griddled trout with ginger and lime drizzle

100 Trout in a paper bag

Preparation time:
10 minutes

Cooking time:
8 minutes

Serves: **4**

4 trout fillets, about 175 g (6 oz) each
3.5 cm (1½ inch) piece of fresh root
  ginger, peeled and finely chopped
1 chilli, finely chopped
1 garlic clove, crushed
grated rind and juice of 3 limes
coriander sprig, to garnish

TO SERVE:
250 g (8 oz) cooked rice noodles
stir-fried mixed vegetables (optional)

Heat a griddle pan. Fold the trout fillets in half lengthways, skin side out, and secure with cocktail sticks. Put the trout on the griddle and cook for 4 minutes on each side.

Meanwhile, mix together the ginger, chilli, garlic and lime rind and juice in a small bowl.

Remove the cocktail sticks from the trout. Serve the fillets on a bed of rice noodles with the lime drizzle poured over the top, garnished with coriander. Accompany with stir-fried mixed vegetables, if liked.

Preparation time:
20 minutes

Cooking time:
20 minutes

Oven temperature:
190°C (375°F) Gas Mark 5

Serves: **4**

4 whole trout, about 125 g (4 oz) each,
  cleaned
2 garlic cloves, finely chopped
1 tablespoon chopped thyme
1 tablespoon chopped rosemary
150 ml (¼ pint) rosé wine
salt and pepper

Cut 8 rectangles of greaseproof paper or foil double the width of each trout and half as long again.

Put 4 of the rectangles on a baking sheet. Lay a trout along the centre of each one, pull up the edges of the paper or foil and fold at each corner so that the paper or foil forms a container for the fish. Sprinkle a little salt and pepper, the garlic and herbs over each trout, then spoon 2 tablespoons of the wine over each one. Cover loosely with the remaining paper or foil and fold at the corners as before to form a lid over the fish. Fold the top and bottom layers of paper or foil together in several places.

Bake the trout in a preheated oven, 190°C (375°F), Gas Mark 5, for 20 minutes until the fish is cooked. Take the fish to the table in the parcels to serve.

NUTRITIONAL INFORMATION It is recommended that we eat up to 4 portions of oily fish per week – at a frequency greater than this, the risks from dioxins may outweigh the benefits. Pregnant or breast-feeding women should limit their intake to twice weekly.

477 kcals (1994 kj) ▪ **low fat** ▪ **low GI** ▪ **source of omega-3 fatty acids** ▪ **source of vitamin C**

189 kcals (792 kj) ▪ **low fat** ▪ **low carb** ▪ **low GI** ▪ **source of omega-3 fatty acids**

101 Spicy crusted swordfish

Preparation time:
10 minutes

Cooking time:
10 minutes

Serves: **4**

4 swordfish fillets, about 175 g (6 oz)
  each, skinned
2 garlic cloves, crushed
1 bunch of coriander, chopped
2 teaspoons paprika
1 teaspoon ground cumin
1 teaspoon finely crushed coriander
  seeds or ground coriander
pinch of dried chilli flakes
1 onion, finely chopped
1 egg white

TO SERVE:
griddled lemon wedges
griddled vegetables
harissa

Pat the swordfish fillets dry with kitchen paper. Mix together the garlic, fresh coriander, paprika, cumin, crushed or ground coriander, chilli flakes and onion. Spread the mixture on a plate.

Tip the egg white into a dish and whisk lightly. Dip the swordfish fillets in the egg white, then into the spice mixture, to coat the fish evenly.

Heat a griddle pan. Put the fish on the griddle and cook for 5 minutes on each side. Serve the swordfish with griddled lemon wedges and vegetables and a little harissa.

249 kcals (1039 kj) ▪ **low fat** ▪ **low carb** ▪ **low GI**

102 Swordfish kebabs with peppers and mango

Preparation time:
20 minutes, plus
marinating

Cooking time:
about 5 minutes

Serves: **4**

500 g (1 lb) swordfish steak, skinned and
  cut into large cubes
1 green pepper, cored, deseeded, and cut
  into 2.5 cm (1 inch) pieces
1 red pepper, cored, deseeded, and cut
  into 2.5 cm (1 inch) pieces
1 red onion, quartered
1 ripe mango, peeled and thickly sliced
rosemary sprig skewers (optional)

MARINADE:
2–3 thyme sprigs
leaves from 1–2 rosemary sprigs
grated rind of 1 lemon
1 garlic clove, lightly crushed
125 ml (4 fl oz) olive oil
2 teaspoons fennel seeds
pepper

Mix together all the marinade ingredients and put into a large, shallow, non-metallic dish with the swordfish cubes, peppers, onion and mango. Cover and leave to marinate at room temperature for about 1 hour.

Heat a griddle pan over a medium heat. Thread the swordfish, peppers, onion and mango on to skewers. If you are using rosemary sprigs as skewers, cover any leaves that are still attached to the ends with a piece of foil to stop them from burning. Put the kebabs on the griddle and cook for about 5 minutes, turning occasionally. Serve immediately.

NUTRITIONAL INFORMATION Roasted red onions contain toxin-removing quercetin and sulphur amino acid. They are considered highly beneficial for their antiviral and antibiotic properties.

585 kcals (2445 kj) ▪ **low carb** ▪ **low GI** ▪ **source of antioxidants** ▪ **source of vitamin C**

Preparation time:
**15 minutes, plus
marinating and infusing**

Cooking time:
4–6 minutes

Serves: **4**

4 swordfish steaks, about 150 g (5 oz) each
4 tablespoons olive oil
1 tablespoon chopped parsley
1 teaspoon thyme leaves
1 garlic clove, crushed
finely grated rind of 1 lime
salt and pepper
baby spinach, to serve

RAW MANGO CHUTNEY:
1 large ripe but firm mango
½ small red onion, finely chopped
**1 small red pepper, cored, deseeded and
   finely chopped**
1 spring onion, finely shredded
1 tablespoon chopped flat leaf parsley
3 tablespoons lime juice
2 tablespoons olive oil

Put the swordfish steaks into a shallow non-metallic bowl. Mix together the oil, parsley, thyme, garlic, lime rind and salt and pepper to taste. Pour over the swordfish, cover and leave to marinate at room temperature for 30 minutes–1 hour.

Meanwhile, to make the chutney, slice the mango lengthways either side of the thin central stone. Remove the skin and discard, then finely dice the flesh and put it into a bowl. Add the remaining ingredients and gently mix together. Cover and leave at room temperature for 1 hour to allow the flavours to infuse.

Heat a grill or griddle pan and cook the swordfish for 2–3 minutes on each side, depending on the thickness of the fish. To serve, put a pile of uncooked baby spinach on each plate, put the hot swordfish steaks on top and spoon the mango chutney over and around them.

439 kcals (1835 kj) ■ **low carb** ■ **low GI** ■ **source of antioxidants**

Preparation time:
5 minutes

Cooking time:
8 minutes

Serves: **4**

**4 red snapper fillets, about 175 g (6 oz)
   each**
1 teaspoon pumpkin seeds
1 teaspoon sunflower seeds
2 teaspoons olive oil
**1 bunch of spring onions, shredded,
   to garnish**
steamed spinach leaves, to serve

Heat a griddle pan. Put the red snapper fillets on the griddle and cook for 4 minutes on each side.

Meanwhile, toss together the salad leaves, pumpkin and sunflower seeds and oil. Serve the snapper fillets with the steamed spinach leaves, garnished with the shredded spring onion.

NUTRITIONAL INFORMATION This recipe is packed with healthy fats – fish, seeds and olive oil provide monounsaturated fat that help to increase 'good' HDL cholesterol, lower 'bad' LDL cholesterol and therefore lower total cholesterol.

234 kcals (983 kj) ■ **low fat** ■ **low carb** ■ **low GI**

105 Sea bass with mushroom stuffing

106 Griddled sea bass with tarragon pesto

Preparation time:
15 minutes

Cooking time:
about 40 minutes

Oven temperature:
200°C (400°F) Gas Mark 6

Serves: **2**

1 tablespoon olive oil
125 g (4 oz) mixed mushrooms, preferably wild, sliced
grated rind and juice of 1 lemon
handful of mixed herbs (such as flat leaf parsley, thyme and green or purple basil), roughly chopped, plus extra to garnish
14 tiny new potatoes
1 garlic clove, crushed
2 sea bass fillets, about 125 g (4 oz) each
pepper

Preparation time:
10 minutes

Cooking time:
8 minutes

Serves: **4**

4 sea bass fillets, about 175 g (6 oz) each
tarragon sprigs, to garnish

TARRAGON PESTO:
50 g (2 oz) pine nuts
1 bunch of tarragon
1 bunch of flat leaf parsley
1 shallot, chopped
1 garlic clove, crushed
50 g (2 oz) walnuts
5 tablespoons olive oil

TO SERVE:
steamed or boiled new potatoes
tomato wedges
purple basil

Heat 1 teaspoon of the oil in a nonstick frying pan and gently fry the mushrooms for about 5 minutes until tender. Season to taste with pepper. Remove the pan from the heat and stir in the lemon rind and juice and the mixed herbs.

Meanwhile, cook the potatoes in boiling water or a steamer for about 10 minutes until just tender. Drain and allow to cool. Put the potatoes into a roasting tin with the garlic, brush with most of the remaining oil and roast in a preheated oven, 200°C (400°F), Gas Mark 6, for about 20 minutes, until golden brown.

Make a crisscross cut on the skin side of each fillet, to prevent the fish from curling up. Make a deep cut lengthways along the side of each fillet and prise open, to make a pocket for the stuffing. Brush the fillets with the remaining oil and stuff with the mushroom and herb mixture. Close the pockets to return the fish to their original shape.

Season the fillets with pepper and put them on top of the potatoes. Return the dish to the oven and bake for 5–6 minutes, depending on size, until the fish is cooked through.

Serve the fish on top of the potatoes, garnished with chopped herbs.

Heat a griddle pan. Fold the sea bass fillets in half lengthways, skin side out (or remove the skin), and secure with cocktail sticks. Put the sea bass on the griddle and cook for 4 minutes on each side, taking care when turning them over.

Meanwhile, to make the pesto, heat a dry frying pan until hot, add the pine nuts and toast lightly, shaking the pan frequently. Put the toasted pine nuts, tarragon, parsley, shallot, garlic, walnuts and oil into a food processor or blender. Whiz for 10 seconds for a rough-textured pesto and slightly longer for a smooth one. Alternatively, pound all the ingredients together using a pestle and mortar.

Remove the cocktail sticks and serve the griddled sea bass with generous amounts of pesto, accompanied by steamed or boiled new potatoes, tomato wedges and purple basil. Garnish with sprigs of tarragon.

257 kcals (1080 kj) ■ low fat ■ source of iron ■ source of protein

519 kcals (2169 kj) ■ low carb ■ low GI ■ source of protein

107 Griddled scallops in their shells

108 Scallops with roasted tomatoes and pancetta

Preparation time:
10 minutes

Cooking time:
2–4 minutes

Serves: **4**

12 large raw scallops, shelled (4 shells reserved) and cleaned
4 tablespoons lime juice
olive oil infused with chilli and garlic, for drizzling
salt and pepper

TO GARNISH:
thin strips of lime rind
finely sliced chillies (optional)

Heat a griddle pan. Pat the scallops dry with kitchen paper. Put the scallops on the griddle and cook for 1–2 minutes on each side. Remove them from the pan. Do not over-cook them or they will become tough.

Divide the scallops between 4 cleaned scallop shells or small serving plates. Drizzle with the lime juice and a little chilli and garlic oil, and season to taste with salt and pepper. Garnish with lime rind strips and sliced chillies, if liked.

Preparation time:
10 minutes

Cooking time:
about 1½ hours

Oven temperature:
110°C (225°F) Gas Mark ¼

Serves: **4**

8 small vine tomatoes, halved
2 garlic cloves, finely chopped
8 basil leaves
2 tablespoons olive oil
2 tablespoons balsamic vinegar
8 thin slices of pancetta
16–20 raw king scallops, shelled, cleaned and corals removed
8 canned artichoke hearts in oil, halved
500 g (1 lb) lamb's lettuce
salt and pepper

Arrange the tomatoes, cut side up, close together in a roasting tin. Scatter with the garlic and basil, drizzle with half the oil and vinegar and season well with salt and pepper. Bake in a preheated oven, 110°C (225°F), Gas Mark ¼, for 1½ hours.

Meanwhile, heat a griddle pan over a high heat. Put the pancetta slices on the griddle and cook for about 2 minutes, turning once, until crisp and golden. Transfer to a plate lined with kitchen paper until needed.

Keeping the griddle pan hot, quickly sear the scallops for 1 minute, then turn them over and cook for a further 1 minute on the other side, or until cooked and starting to caramelize. Remove the scallops from the pan, cover with foil and allow to rest for 2 minutes while you griddle the artichoke hearts until hot and charred.

Toss the lamb's lettuce with the remaining oil and vinegar and arrange on warmed plates. Top with the artichokes, tomatoes and cooked scallops. Crumble the pancetta over the top and serve immediately.

218 kcals (917 kj) ■ **low carb** ■ **low GI** ■ **source of protein** ■ **source of vitamin B**

257 kcals (1074 kj) ■ **low carb** ■ **low GI** ■ **source of antioxidants** ■ **source of potassium**

109 Portuguese cod

110 Blackened cod with citrus salsa

Preparation time:
10 minutes

Cooking time:
30–35 minutes

Oven temperature:
180°C (350°F) Gas Mark 4

Serves: **4**

25 g (1 oz) low-fat spread
1 onion, chopped
1 garlic clove, crushed
4 tomatoes, skinned and chopped
juice of 1 lemon
4 cod fillets, about 200 g (7 oz) each
salt and pepper
chopped parsley, to garnish
steamed asparagus, to serve (optional)

Preparation time:
15 minutes, plus infusing

Cooking time:
15 minutes

Oven temperature:
150°C (300°F) Gas Mark 2

Serves: **4**

4 cod fillets, about 175 g (6 oz) each
1 tablespoon olive oil
1 tablespoon jerk seasoning
salt and pepper
green salad, to serve

CITRUS SALSA:
1 large orange
1 garlic clove, crushed
2 large tomatoes, skinned, deseeded and diced
2 tablespoons chopped basil, plus extra to garnish
50 g (2 oz) pitted black olives, chopped
4 tablespoons olive oil
salt and pepper

Heat the low-fat spread in a saucepan and fry the onion until soft but not brown. Add the garlic, tomatoes and lemon juice. Season to taste with salt and pepper and stir well.

Spoon about one-third of this sauce into a shallow ovenproof dish. Arrange the cod fillets on top, then pour over the remaining sauce. Cover the dish with a lid or a piece of foil and bake in a preheated oven, 190°C (375°F), Gas Mark 5, for 25–30 minutes.

Remove the cod from the oven and sprinkle with a little chopped parsley. Serve with steamed asparagus, if liked.

To make the salsa, remove the rind and pith from the orange. Working over a bowl to catch the juice, cut between the membranes to remove the segments. Halve the segments and mix them with the reserved orange juice, garlic, tomatoes, basil, olives and oil. Season to taste with salt and pepper, cover and set aside to infuse.

Brush the cod fillets with the oil and coat with the jerk seasoning. Heat a large heavy-based frying pan and fry the cod fillets, skin side down, for 5 minutes. Turn them over and cook them for a further 3 minutes. Transfer the fillets to a preheated oven, 150°C (300°F), Gas Mark 2, to rest for about 5 minutes. Garnish the fish with basil and serve with the salsa and a green salad.

COOK'S NOTES Cod is particularly low in fat. It has a moist, firm, creamy-white flesh, which flakes when it is cooked. It is extremely versatile and can be prepared in many different ways. However, prolonged cooking harms both the flavour and the presentation.

192 kcals (805 kj) ■ low fat ■ low carb ■ low GI ■ source of iron ■ source of protein

353 kcals (1476 kj) ■ low carb ■ low GI ■ source of iron ■ source of protein

111 Cod fillets with a herb crust

Preparation time:
15 minutes

Cooking time:
20 minutes

Oven temperature:
180°C (350°F) Gas Mark 4

Serves: 4

4 cod fillets, about 125 g (4 oz) each
50 g (2 oz) wholemeal breadcrumbs
2 tablespoons chopped dill
2 tablespoons chopped parsley
2 tablespoons snipped chives
2 tablespoons low-fat fromage frais
2 plum tomatoes, finely diced
2 tablespoons lemon juice
salt and pepper

TO SERVE:
steamed whole green beans
cooked tagliatelle

Pat the cod fillets dry with kitchen paper and season to taste with salt and pepper. Put them into a foil-lined roasting tin, skin side down.

To make the herb crust, mix together all the remaining ingredients in a bowl and spoon some on top of each cod fillet, packing the mixture down gently.

Cook the cod fillets in a preheated oven, 180°C (350°F), Gas Mark 4, for 20 minutes, covering the tin with foil if the crust is getting too brown. Serve with whole green beans and tagliatelle.

140 kcals (585 kj) ■ **low fat** ■ **low carb** ■ **low GI** ■ **source of iron** ■ **source of protein**

112 Griddled miso cod with pak choi

Preparation time:
10 minutes, plus cooling
and marinating

Cooking time:
15–20 minutes

Serves: 4

4 chunky cod fillets, about 175 g (6 oz)
each
4 heads pak choi, halved lengthways
and blanched in boiling water for 1–2
minutes
olive oil, for brushing

MISO SAUCE:
125 g (4 oz) miso paste
125 ml (4 fl oz) soy sauce
125 ml (4 fl oz) sake
125 ml (4 fl oz) rice wine (mirin)
50 g (2 oz) sugar

First, to make the miso sauce, put all the ingredients into a small saucepan and heat gently until the sugar has dissolved. Simmer very gently for about 5 minutes, stirring frequently. Remove from the heat and allow to cool.

Arrange the cod fillets in a snug-fitting dish and cover with the cold miso sauce. Rub the sauce over the fillets so that they are completely covered, cover and leave to marinate in the refrigerator for at least 6 hours, preferably overnight.

Heat a griddle pan over a medium heat. Remove the cod fillets from the miso sauce, put them on the griddle and cook for about 2–3 minutes, then carefully turn them over and cook for a further 2–3 minutes. Remove them from the pan and keep warm.

Heat the cleaned griddle pan and brush a little oil over the cut side of the pak choi. Put the pak choi, cut side down, on the griddle and cook for about 2 minutes until hot and lightly charred. Arrange on a warmed serving plate with the cod and serve immediately.

341 kcals (1425 kj) ■ **low fat** ■ **low carb** ■ **source of iron** ■ **source of protein**

113 Cod with sweet potato and spinach mash

Preparation time:
15 minutes

Cooking time:
15 minutes

Serves: **4**

1 kg (2 lb) sweet potatoes, peeled and roughly cubed
175 g (6 oz) baby spinach, torn
2 tablespoons olive oil
1 tablespoon crushed mixed peppercorns
4 thick cod fillets, about 150 g (5 oz) each
salt and pepper

Steam the sweet potato cubes in a steamer over boiling water for 10–15 minutes, or until just soft. While they are still hot, transfer the sweet potatoes to a bowl and mash roughly.

Add the torn spinach leaves, oil and salt and pepper to taste and mix together. If the sweet potato is still hot, the spinach leaves will wilt into the mash. Cover and keep warm.

Meanwhile, mix some salt with the crushed peppercorns and sprinkle over one side of the cod fillets.

Cook the fish, peppered side up, under a preheated hot grill for 8–10 minutes, or until they are cooked through. Serve the cod on a bed of sweet potato and spinach mash.

NUTRITIONAL INFORMATION Sweet potatoes are full of antioxidants, particularly vitamins A, C and E. Choose darker-coloured potatoes for the highest amount of these antioxidants. Like yams and new potatoes, sweet potatoes take longer to digest than other potatoes and help to lower the overall glycaemic index (GI) of the diet.

417 kcals (1743 kj) ▪ low fat ▪ low GI ▪ source of iron ▪ source of protein ▪ source of vitamins A, C and E

114 Fish pie

Preparation time:
15 minutes

Cooking time:
20 minutes

Serves: **6**

750 g (1½ lb) cod or haddock fillets, or a mixture of white fish
300 ml (½ pint) semi-skimmed milk, plus about 150 ml (¼ pint) hot semi-skimmed milk
1 bay leaf
½ onion, sliced
6 peppercorns
25 g (1 oz) butter or margarine, plus extra for greasing
3 tablespoons flour
2 tablespoons chopped parsley or dill
4 tomatoes, skinned and sliced
1 kg (2 lb) potatoes
salt and freshly ground white pepper

Simmer the fish gently in a saucepan in the 300 ml (½ pint) milk and water to cover, with the bay leaf, onion and peppercorns, until cooked. Strain the fish liquid, measure and make up to 450 ml (¾ pint) with more milk if necessary.

Melt the butter or margarine in a saucepan and stir in the flour. Cook over a gentle heat, stirring, for 1 minute, then stir in the strained fish liquid. Bring to the boil, stirring, and cook until the sauce is smooth and thick. Season to taste with salt and pepper and stir in the chopped parsley or dill. Pour a little of the sauce into a greased ovenproof dish and put the fish on top. Cover with the sliced tomatoes and pour over the remaining sauce.

Meanwhile, cook the potatoes in a large saucepan of boiling water until tender, then beat them to a purée with the hot milk. Season to taste with salt and pepper and pile on top of the fish mixture. Brown under a preheated grill for a few minutes before serving.

485 kcals (2027 kj) ▪ low fat ▪ high fibre ▪ source of iron ▪ source of protein

115 Grilled haddock with lentils and spinach

116 Smoked haddock and pea risotto

Preparation time:
5 minutes

Cooking time:
about 10 minutes

Serves: **1**

1 teaspoon olive oil
½ onion, finely chopped
pinch of ground cumin
pinch of turmeric
pinch of dried chilli flakes
⅓ x 400 g (13 oz) can lentils, rinsed and drained
75 g (3 oz) baby spinach
2 tablespoons low-fat crème fraîche
1 piece of boneless, skinless haddock, about 125 g (4 oz)
lemon wedge, to garnish
grilled cherry tomatoes, to serve

Preparation time:
10 minutes

Cooking time:
about 25 minutes

Serves: **4**

1 teaspoon olive oil
1 small onion, finely chopped
350 g (11½ oz) arborio rice
1 small glass dry white wine
900 ml (1½ pints) Vegetable Stock (see Introduction), simmering
350 g (11½ oz) smoked haddock fillet, skinned and cubed
200 g (7 oz) frozen peas
2 tablespoons snipped chives
3 tablespoons freshly grated Parmesan cheese, plus extra to serve (optional)
pepper

Heat half the oil in a nonstick frying pan and fry the onion for 3–4 minutes until softened. Add the cumin, turmeric and chilli flakes and fry for 1 minute. Stir in the lentils, spinach and crème fraîche and cook gently for 3 minutes until the spinach has wilted.

Meanwhile, brush the haddock on each side with the remaining oil. Put the haddock on a nonstick baking sheet and cook under a preheated hot grill for 2–3 minutes on each side until done. To serve, arrange the lentils and spinach on a plate and top with the haddock. Garnish with a lemon wedge and serve with grilled cherry tomatoes.

Heat the oil in a large nonstick frying pan and fry the onion for 2–3 minutes until it begins to soften. Add the rice and cook, stirring, for 1 minute. Add the wine and cook, stirring, until it has been absorbed.

Reduce the heat and add the stock, a ladleful at a time, stirring constantly, allowing each ladleful to be absorbed before adding the next. Add the haddock and peas with the last ladleful of stock and cook for a further 5 minutes, or until the fish flakes easily and the rice is creamy but still firm to the bite. The whole process will take about 20 minutes.

Stir in the remaining ingredients and season well with pepper. Serve with extra grated Parmesan, if liked.

360 kcals (1512 kj) ■ **low fat** ■ **source of iron** ■ **source of omega-3 fatty acids** ■ **source of protein**

496 kcals (2100 kj) ■ **low fat** ■ **low GI** ■ **high fibre** ■ **source of omega-3 fatty acids**

117 Sesame tuna with dipping sauce

118 Griddled honey-glazed tuna with parsnip purée

Preparation time:
10 minutes

Cooking time:
8–18 minutes

Serves: **4**

575 g (1 lb 3 oz) tuna fillet, or 2 fillets, about 300 g (10 oz) each, skinned
3 tablespoons black sesame seeds
3 tablespoons white sesame seeds
1 egg white
salt
cooked spinach, to serve

DIPPING SAUCE:
100 ml (3½ fl oz) soy sauce
1 chilli, finely chopped
1 garlic clove, crushed

Preparation time:
15 minutes

Cooking time:
20 minutes

Serves: **4**

4 tuna steaks, about 125 g (4 oz) each
2 teaspoons olive oil
steamed whole green beans, to serve

GLAZE:
1 tablespoon clear honey
2 tablespoons wholegrain mustard
1 teaspoon tomato purée
2 tablespoons orange juice
1 tablespoon red wine vinegar
pepper

PARSNIP PURÉE:
2 parsnips, cut into chunks
2 potatoes, cut into chunks
50 g (2 oz) low-fat natural yogurt
2 teaspoons horseradish relish (optional)

Toast the sesame seeds by dry-frying them in a frying pan until they begin to jump vigorously.

Pat the tuna dry with kitchen paper. Mix together the black and white sesame seeds and pour on to a plate. Tip the egg white into a dish and whisk lightly.

Dip the tuna in the egg white, then into the toasted sesame seeds and pat them on to the tuna, to coat the fish thoroughly.

Heat a griddle pan. Slice the tuna diagonally. Put the tuna slices on the griddle and cook for 3 minutes on each side for rare, 5 minutes for medium or 8 minutes for well done.

Meanwhile, to make the dipping sauce, mix together all the ingredients and pour into 4 little dishes. Season the tuna slices to taste with salt, then serve on individual plates with cooked spinach and with the sauce served separately.

Put all the ingredients for the glaze into a small saucepan. Bring to the boil, then reduce the heat and simmer until the mixture reduces and has a light and syrupy consistency. Keep hot.

To make the parsnip purée, steam the parsnips and potatoes until tender. Drain if necessary, put into a food processor or blender with the yogurt, horseradish, if using, and pepper to taste and whiz until blended. Keep warm or reheat prior to serving.

Brush the tuna with the oil. Cook on a preheated, very hot griddle, or in a frying pan or under a grill, for 1–2 minutes. Turn the tuna over and spoon some of the glaze over it. Cook for a further 1–2 minutes – tuna is best if it is moist and still slightly pink in the centre. To serve, pile a mound of the parsnip purée on each plate, top with a tuna steak and spoon over the remaining glaze. Serve with steamed green beans.

297 kcals (1242 kj) ■ **low carb** ■ **low GI** ■ **source of iron** ■ **source of omega-3 fatty acids**

337 kcals (1414 kj) ■ **low fat** ■ **source of omega-3 fatty acids** ■ **source of protein**

Preparation time:
10 minutes

Cooking time:
4–6 minutes

Serves: **2**

2 fresh tuna steaks, about 150 g (5 oz) each
1 tablespoon olive oil
salt and pepper
lime wedges, to garnish

AVOCADO SALSA:
1 large ripe avocado, stoned, peeled and diced
4 ripe plum tomatoes, quartered deseeded and diced
1 small red onion, finely chopped
300 g (10 oz) canned black-eyed beans, drained and rinsed
2 tablespoons chopped coriander
grated rind and juice of 1 lime

To make the salsa, mix together the avocado, tomatoes, onion and beans in a large bowl. Stir in the coriander, lime rind and juice and salt and pepper to taste. Set aside.

Brush the tuna with the oil. Cook on a preheated, very hot griddle, or in a frying pan or under a grill, for 2–3 minutes on each side, or until cooked to your liking. Transfer the tuna to warmed serving plates, garnish with lime wedges and serve with the salsa.

Preparation time:
15 minutes

Cooking time:
20–25 minutes

Oven temperature:
220°C (425°F) Gas Mark 7

Serves: **4**

2 red peppers, cored, deseeded and roughly chopped
6 plum tomatoes, skinned and roughly chopped
2 celery sticks, roughly chopped
3 large garlic cloves
1 tablespoon olive oil
8 small plaice fillets, total weight about 500 g (1 lb)
4 teaspoons ready-made fresh pesto
150 ml (¼ pint) dry white wine
pepper
tender-stem broccoli, to serve (optional)

Put the peppers, tomatoes, celery and garlic into a large roasting tin, drizzle with the oil and season to taste with pepper. Cook in a preheated oven, 220°C (425°F), Gas Mark 7, for 15–20 minutes, or until the vegetables are soft.

Meanwhile, remove the skin from the plaice fillets, then put the fish, skinned side uppermost, on a board. Spread each one with 1 teaspoon pesto and roll up the fillets as you would a Swiss roll.

Pour the wine into a flameproof casserole and add the rolled fish, seam side down. Bring the wine to the boil, then cover the pan with a lid or a piece of foil, reduce the heat and leave to simmer for about 10 minutes. Using a slotted spoon, transfer the fish to a warmed serving dish. Reserve the wine.

Put the roasted vegetables and the wine into a food processor or blender and whiz for 2–3 minutes until smooth. Return the sauce to the pan, reheat and season to taste with salt and pepper. Serve as an accompaniment to the fish, with tender-stem broccoli, if liked.

595 kcals (2499 kj) ■ **low carb** ■ **low GI** ■ **high fibre** ■ **source of antioxidants** ■ **source of omega-3 fatty acids**

194 kcals (811 kj) ■ **low fat** ■ **low carb** ■ **low GI** ■ **source of antioxidants**

121 Lemon sole stuffed with wild mushrooms

122 Zarzuela with mussels, calamari and cod

Preparation time: **20 minutes**	**5 g (¼ oz) butter** **125 g (4 oz) wild mushrooms (such as chanterelles), roughly chopped or torn**
Cooking time: **25 minutes**	**dash of Worcestershire sauce** **25 g (1 oz) sun-dried tomato paste** **25 g (1 oz) watercress leaves**
Oven temperature: **200°C (400°F) Gas Mark 6**	**4 lemon sole fillets, about 75 g (3 oz) each, skinned** **3 tablespoons white wine**
Serves: **4**	**salt and pepper** **dill sprigs, to garnish**

TO SERVE:
boiled new potatoes (optional)
boiled carrots (optional)

Preparation time: **30 minutes**	**1 tablespoon olive oil** **1 large onion, finely chopped** **2 garlic cloves, finely chopped**
Cooking time: **about 25 minutes**	**½ teaspoon pimenton (smoked paprika)** **500 g (1 lb) tomatoes, skinned and chopped**
Serves: **4**	**1 red pepper, cored, deseeded and diced** **200 ml (7 fl oz) Fish Stock (see Introduction)** **150 ml (¼ pint) dry white wine** **2 large pinches of saffron threads** **4 small bay leaves** **500 g (1 lb) live mussels** **200 g (7 oz) cleaned calamari, rinsed** **375 g (12 oz) cod loin, skinned** **salt and pepper**

Melt the butter in a saucepan and fry the mushrooms until softened. Add the Worcestershire sauce and sun-dried tomato paste and cook for a further few minutes. Stir in the watercress leaves and cook until the leaves are wilted, then remove the pan from the heat. Season well with salt and pepper.

Put the sole fillets on a work surface, skinned side uppermost, and divide the filling between them. Starting at the narrowest point, roll up each fillet to enclose the stuffing and secure with a cocktail stick. Arrange the fish, seam side down, in a small roasting tin. Add the wine, season again and cover the tin with foil.

Cook the sole in a preheated oven, 200°C (400°F), Gas Mark 6, for 12 minutes or until they are just opaque. Serve garnished with dill sprigs and accompanied by boiled new potatoes and carrots, if liked.

Heat the oil in a large saucepan and fry the onion for 5 minutes until softened. Stir in the garlic and pimenton and cook for 1 minute. Stir in the tomatoes, pepper, stock, wine and saffron. Add the bay leaves, season to taste with salt and pepper and bring to the boil. Cover the pan and simmer gently for 10 minutes. Set aside until needed.

Discard any mussels that are broken or do not close immediately when sharply tapped with a knife. Scrub the shells with a stiff brush, remove any barnacles and pull off the tuft-like beards. Put the mussels into a bowl of clean water. Separate the calamari tubes from the tentacles and slice the tubes into rings. Cut the cod into cubes.

Reheat the tomato sauce if necessary. Add the cod and the calamari rings and cook for 2 minutes. Add the mussels, cover the pan and cook for 4 minutes. Add the calamari tentacles and cook for 2 minutes until they are cooked through and all the mussels have opened. Discard any that remain closed. Stir gently, spoon into bowls and serve.

99 kcals (415 kj) ▪ low fat ▪ low carb ▪ low GI ▪
source of potassium ▪ **source of protein**

242 kcals (1020 kj) ▪ low fat ▪ low carb ▪ low GI ▪
source of iron ▪ **source of protein**

123 Lime, coconut and chilli-spiked squid

124 Mussel and lemon curry

Preparation time:
10 minutes, plus marinating

Cooking time:
about 5 minutes

Serves: **2**

10–12 cleaned baby squid, total weight about 375 g (12 oz) including tentacles

DRESSING:
2 red chillies, finely chopped
juice and grated rind of 2 limes
2.5 cm (1 inch) piece of fresh root ginger, peeled and grated
40 g (¾ oz) dried, creamed or freshly grated coconut
4 tablespoons groundnut oil
1–2 tablespoons chilli oil
1 tablespoon white wine vinegar

TO SERVE:
4 limes, halved
mixed green salad

Cut down the side of each squid so that they can be laid flat. Using a sharp knife, score the inside flesh lightly in a crisscross pattern.

Mix together all the dressing ingredients. Toss the squid in half the dressing, cover and leave to marinate at room temperature for about 1 hour.

Heat a griddle pan over a high heat. Put the limes, cut side down, on the griddle and cook for about 2 minutes until nicely charred. Set aside. Keeping the griddle very hot, add the squid to the pan and cook quickly for 1 minute. Turn them over and cook for a further 1 minute until they are charred.

Cut the squid into strips. Put on a warmed serving platter and top with the remaining dressing. Serve with the griddled limes and a mixed green salad.

Preparation time:
15 minutes

Cooking time:
15 minutes

Serves: **4**

1 kg (2 lb) live mussels
125 ml (4 fl oz) lager
125 g (4 oz) unsalted butter
1 onion, chopped
1 garlic clove, crushed
2.5 cm (1 inch) piece of fresh root ginger, peeled and grated
1 tablespoon medium curry powder
150 ml (¼ pint) single cream
2 tablespoons lemon juice
salt and pepper
chopped parsley, to garnish

Discard any mussels that are broken or do not close immediately when sharply tapped with a knife. Scrub the shells with a stiff brush, remove any barnacles and pull off the tuft-like beards. Put them into a large saucepan with the lager, cover and cook, shaking the pan frequently, for 4 minutes until all the shells have opened. Discard any that remain closed. Strain, reserve the cooking liquid and keep it warm.

Meanwhile, melt the butter in a large saucepan and fry the onion, garlic, ginger and curry powder, stirring frequently, for 5 minutes. Pour in the reserved cooking liquid through a sieve, bring to the boil and boil until reduced by half.

Whisk in the cream and lemon juice and simmer gently. Stir in the mussels, warm through and season to taste with salt and pepper. Garnish with chopped parsley and serve immediately.

318 kcals (1329 kj) ■ **low carb** ■ **low GI** ■ **source of vitamin C**

460 kcals (1933 kj) ■ **low carb** ■ **low GI** ■ **source of omega-3 fatty acids**

125 Lemon and chilli prawn linguine

126 Kerala prawn curry

Preparation time:
15 minutes

Cooking time:
10–12 minutes

Serves: **4**

375 g (12 oz) dried linguine or spaghetti
1 tablespoon olive oil
15 g (½ oz) butter
1 garlic clove, finely chopped
2 spring onions, thinly sliced
2 red chillies, deseeded and thinly sliced
425 g (14 oz) large raw king prawns,
  peeled and deveined but tails left intact
2 tablespoons lemon juice
2 tablespoons finely chopped coriander
  leaves
salt and pepper
coriander leaves, to garnish

Preparation time:
5 minutes

Cooking time:
8 minutes

Serves: **4**

½ teaspoon turmeric
500 g (1 lb) large cooked peeled prawns
1 teaspoon vegetable oil
1 red onion, cut into fine wedges
2 green chillies, deseeded and sliced
10 curry leaves (optional)
100 ml (3½ fl oz) coconut milk
2 tablespoons lime juice
few coriander leaves
salt and pepper
steamed basmati rice, to serve (optional)

Cook the linguine in a large saucepan of lightly salted boiling water for 10–12 minutes, or according to the packet instructions, until al dente. Drain well.

Meanwhile, heat the oil and butter in a large frying pan and stir-fry the garlic, spring onions and chillies for 2–3 minutes. Add the prawns and cook briskly, stirring, for 3–4 minutes, or until they turn pink and are just cooked through.

Stir in the lemon juice and coriander, then remove the pan from the heat. Add the drained pasta, season well with salt and pepper and toss together. Serve immediately, garnished with coriander leaves.

Sprinkle the turmeric over the prawns and set aside. Heat the oil in a wok and stir-fry the onion wedges and chillies until softened.

Add the prawns, curry leaves, if using, and coconut milk and simmer for 5 minutes.

Sprinkle the lime juice over the curry and season to taste with salt and pepper. Scatter with coriander leaves and stir once. Serve immediately with steamed basmati rice, if liked.

NUTRITIONAL INFORMATION Prawns were once considered off-limits for those with cholesterol problems, because they contain dietary cholesterol. It is now known, however, that saturated fat, not dietary cholesterol, has the greater impact on blood cholesterol levels.

436 kcals (1829 kj) ▪ **low fat** ▪ **low GI** ▪ **source of vitamin C**

194 kcals (814 kj) ▪ **low fat** ▪ **low carb** ▪ **low GI** ▪ **source of antioxidants**

127 Chilli prawns with lime basmati

128 King prawns with pineapple

Preparation time:
15 minutes

Cooking time:
12–15 minutes

Serves: **4**

450 g (14½ oz) raw king prawns, peeled and deveined
2 garlic cloves, crushed
2 fresh red chillies, finely chopped
2 tablespoons chopped coriander leaves
1 teaspoon sesame oil
grated rind and juice of 2 limes (reserve 2 of the lime 'shells')
225 g (7½ oz) basmati rice, rinsed
350 ml (12 fl oz) boiling water, plus 4 tablespoons water
25 g (1 oz) creamed coconut

TO GARNISH:
25 g (1 oz) peanuts, crushed, (optional)
lime wedges

Put the prawns into a non-metallic bowl. Put the garlic, chillies, coriander, oil and half the lime rind and juice into a mortar and grind with a pestle to make a paste, or use a food processor. Tip the mixture over the prawns and stir, covering the prawns with the paste.

Put the rice into a saucepan and pour over the measurement water, the lime 'shells' and the remaining lime rind and juice. Bring to the boil, then reduce the heat, cover the pan and simmer for 12–15 minutes until the liquid is absorbed and the rice is tender and fluffy. Remove the lime 'shells' and discard.

Meanwhile, heat a dry frying pan until hot, then add the prawns and fry for 2–3 minutes until they just turn pink. Add the coconut and 4 tablespoons water and bring to the boil, then reduce the heat and simmer for 1 minute. Serve the prawns with the rice, garnished with peanuts, if liked, and lime wedges.

Preparation time:
15 minutes

Cooking time:
10 minutes

Serves: **4**

1 pineapple, peeled and cored
12 tarragon sprigs
12 raw king prawns, heads removed, peeled and deveined but tails left intact

Cut the pineapple lengthways into long thin slices.

Heat a griddle pan. Put a tarragon sprig on top of each prawn and wrap them in a thin ribbon of pineapple. Secure with a cocktail stick.

Put the wrapped prawns on the griddle and cook for 5 minutes on each side. Serve the prawns hot or cold.

NUTRITIONAL INFORMATION Pineapple contains the enzyme bromelain, which helps digestion by aiding the breakdown of protein.

772 kcals (3227 kj) ■ **low GI** ■ **source of vitamin C**

85 kcals (355 kj) ■ **low carb** ■ **low GI** ■ **source of antioxidants**

6 Poultry and Game

Preparation time:
15 minutes, plus cooling

Cooking time:
1¾–2¼ hours

Serves: 8

2 kg (4 lb) oven-ready chicken
1 onion, quartered
1 carrot, sliced
2 celery sticks, sliced
4 juniper berries, crushed
1 bay leaf
4–6 parsley stalks
salt
6 peppercorns, lightly crushed
chopped parsley, to garnish
griddled courgette slices, to serve

SAUCE:
250 g (8 oz) bottled pimientos, rinsed,
drained and chopped
1 tablespoon tomato purée
2 tablespoons mango chutney
200 ml (7 fl oz) low-fat natural yogurt
salt and pepper

Put the chicken, vegetables, juniper berries, bay leaf, parsley, salt to taste and peppercorns into a saucepan, cover with water and bring to the boil. Reduce the heat, cover the pan and simmer for 1½–2 hours, or until the chicken is tender. Leave it to cool in the stock, then lift it out, drain and dry. Reserve the stock. Skin the chicken and slice the meat.

To make the sauce, put the pimientos, 2 tablespoons of the reserved stock, the tomato purée and chutney into a saucepan and bring to the boil. Transfer the mixture to a food processor or blender and whiz until smooth. Allow to cool, then blend the cooled mixture with the yogurt and season to taste with salt and pepper.

Arrange the chicken on a warmed serving dish and pour over the sauce. Serve with griddled courgettes and garnish with chopped parsley.

Preparation time:
10 minutes

Cooking time:
20 minutes

Serves: 4

4 boneless, skinless chicken breasts,
about 125 g (4 oz) each
coriander leaves, to garnish
cooked rice noodles, to serve

CHILLI JAM:
125 g (4 oz) fresh chillies, deseeded and
chopped
1 garlic clove, crushed
1 onion, chopped
5 cm (2 inch) piece of fresh root ginger,
peeled and chopped
125 ml (4 fl oz) white vinegar
500 g (1 lb) sugar

First, to make the chilli jam, put all the ingredients into a small saucepan. Bring to the boil, then reduce the heat and simmer for 15 minutes. The mixture should be thick, sticky and jam-like, and will become more so as it cools.

Meanwhile, heat a griddle pan. Put the chicken breasts on the griddle, skin side down, and cook for 10 minutes, then turn them over and cook for a further 10 minutes.

Serve the chicken on a bed of rice noodles, with the chilli jam poured over the top, garnished with coriander. Store any remaining chilli jam in the refrigerator, covered, for up to 1 week, and use it as an accompaniment to spice up other griddled or grilled meats.

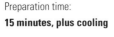

401 kcals (1676 kj) ▪ low carb ▪ low GI

705 kcals (2947 kj) ▪ low fat ▪ source of vitamin C

131 Chicken breasts with lime and ginger

132 Spinach-stuffed chicken breasts

Preparation time:
10 minutes, plus standing

Cooking time:
20–30 minutes

Serves: **4**

4 boneless, skinless chicken breasts, about 150 g (5 oz) each
1 lime, halved and thinly sliced
2.5 cm (1 inch) piece of fresh root ginger, peeled and grated
2 tablespoons light soy sauce
2 tablespoons dry sherry
1 red chilli, deseeded and finely sliced
flat leaf parsley sprigs, to garnish
steamed vegetables, to serve

Make a few deep cuts in the chicken, but do not to cut all the way through the breasts. Push a slice of lime into each slit and put the chicken on a grill rack.

Mix together the ginger, soy sauce, sherry and chilli in a bowl. Brush some of the marinade over each chicken breast, cover and leave to stand for 10 minutes.

Cook the chicken breasts under a preheated medium grill for 20–30 minutes, turning once, or until the juices run clear, covering the meat with foil if necessary to prevent it from over-browning. Warm the remaining marinade and drizzle over the chicken before serving. Garnish with flat leaf parsley and serve with steamed vegetables.

Preparation time:
20 minutes

Cooking time:
55 minutes

Oven temperature:
190°C (375°F) Gas Mark 5

Serves: **4**

125 g (4 oz) fresh spinach
50 g (2 oz) low fat cream cheese or fromage frais
1 onion, grated
1 teaspoon grated lemon rind
50 g (2 oz) chestnut mushrooms, finely chopped
4 skinless chicken breasts, about 150 g (5 oz) each
1 large potato, parboiled
salt and pepper
roasted red onions and tomatoes, to serve (optional)

Put the fresh spinach and cream cheese or fromage frais into a food processor or blender and whiz until smooth. Season well with salt and pepper and transfer to a bowl.

Heat a frying pan and dry-fry the onion for 5 minutes until soft and slightly coloured. Add the lemon rind and mushrooms and fry for 5 minutes to extract the juice from the mushrooms. Stir into the spinach mixture.

Make a deep cut along the length of each chicken breast, and open up to form a pocket. Spoon a little of the spinach mixture into each pocket.

Finely slice the potato and arrange a quarter of the slices in a line in an ovenproof dish, overlapping them slightly. Lift a chicken breast on to the potatoes. Repeat with the remaining potato and the remaining chicken breasts. Season to taste with pepper. Bake in a preheated oven, 190°C (375°F), Gas Mark 5, for 45 minutes, covering the chicken with foil if necessary to prevent it from over-browning. Serve with roasted red onions and tomatoes, if liked.

189 kcals (793 kj) ▪ **low fat** ▪ **low carb** ▪ **low GI** ▪ **source of protein**

225 kcals (945 kj) ▪ **low fat** ▪ **low carb** ▪ **low GI** ▪ **source of antioxidants** ▪ **source of iron**

Preparation time:
15 minutes

Cooking time:
about 15 minutes

Serves: **4**

1 tablespoon olive oil
4 boneless, skinless chicken breasts, about 150 g (5 oz) each
200 g (7 oz) shallots, halved
1 garlic clove, finely chopped
1 apple, cored and diced
75 g (3 oz) button mushrooms, sliced
4 tablespoons Calvados or brandy
250 ml (8 fl oz) Chicken Stock (see Introduction)
1 teaspoon Dijon mustard
1 small bunch of thyme, plus extra to garnish
salt and pepper
cooked sugar snap peas, halved lengthways, to serve (optional)

Heat the oil in a ridged frying pan and fry the chicken breasts and shallots for 4 minutes until the chicken is browned on the underside.

Turn the chicken over and add the garlic, apple and mushrooms. Fry for 6 minutes, or until the chicken is cooked through.

Spoon the Calvados or brandy over the chicken and, when it is bubbling, set alight with a match and stand well back. When the flames subside, add the stock, mustard, thyme and salt and pepper to taste and cook for 5 minutes.

Cut each chicken breast into 4 and arrange the slices on a bed of shallots, apple and mushrooms. Spoon the sauce around and sprinkle with a little extra thyme. Serve with sugar snap peas, halved lengthways, if liked.

Preparation time:
10 minutes

Cooking time:
10 minutes

Serves: **4**

1 tablespoon olive oil
2 boneless, skinless chicken breasts, sliced
2 red onions, cut into wedges
2 red peppers, cored, deseeded and sliced
1 yellow pepper, cored, deseeded and sliced
pinch of dried chilli flakes
2 tablespoons chopped coriander leaves
2 tablespoons lime juice
8 medium flour tortillas
4 tablespoons low-fat crème fraîche
coriander sprigs, to garnish

Heat the oil in a frying pan and fry the chicken slices for 2–3 minutes until they are beginning to brown.

Add the onions, peppers and chilli flakes and fry for a further 5 minutes. Remove the pan from the heat and stir in the coriander and lime juice.

Warm the tortillas according to the packet instructions, then fill them with the chicken mixture and some crème fraîche, garnish with coriander sprigs and serve immediately.

NUTRITIONAL INFORMATION Flour tortillas have a high GI value, so look out for wholegrain versions available in larger super-markets and health-food shops.

328 kcals (1373 kj) ■ low fat ■ low carb ■ low GI ■ source of protein

328 kcals (1373 kj) ■ low fat ■ source of antioxidants

135 Chicken, mushroom and fennel rice

Preparation time: **10 minutes**	**1 tablespoon olive oil**
	1 fennel bulb, trimmed, cored and finely sliced
Cooking time: **30 minutes**	**1 onion, finely sliced**
	1 garlic clove, crushed
	175 g (6 oz) mixed mushrooms, sliced
Serves: **4**	**250 g (8 oz) basmati rice**
	150 ml (¼ pint) dry white wine
	450 ml (¾ pint) Chicken Stock (see Introduction), simmering
	250 g (8 oz) cooked chicken, diced
	½ bunch of dill, finely chopped,
	finely grated rind and juice of 1 lemon
	pepper

TO GARNISH:
25 g (1 oz) pine nuts, toasted
dill sprigs

Heat the oil in a saucepan and gently fry the fennel, onion and garlic for 5 minutes. Add the mushrooms and fry for 2 minutes. Add the rice and cook, stirring, for 1 minute. Add the wine and cook, stirring, until it has been absorbed.

Pour in half the stock and bring it to the boil, then reduce the heat and simmer gently, stirring frequently, until it has been absorbed. Add the remaining stock a ladleful at a time, stirring constantly, allowing each ladleful to be absorbed before adding the next.

Add the chicken, dill and lemon rind and juice with the last ladleful of stock and cook for a further 5 minutes, or until the rice is creamy but still firm to the bite. The whole process will take about 20 minutes. Season to taste with pepper and turn into a warmed serving dish. Sprinkle with toasted pine nuts and garnish with dill sprigs.

423 kcals (1778 kj) ■ **low GI** ■ **source of potassium** ■ **source of protein**

136 Citrus chicken with fruited bulgar wheat

Preparation time: **25 minutes**	**900 ml (1½ pints) Chicken Stock (see Introduction)**
	¼ teaspoon ground cinnamon
Cooking time: **about 15 minutes**	**¼ teaspoon ground nutmeg or allspice**
	250 g (8 oz) bulgar wheat
	4 boneless, skinless chicken breasts, about 150 g (5 oz) each
Serves: **4**	**grated rind of ½ lemon**
	grated rind of ½ orange
	125 g (4 oz) ready-to-eat dried apricots, roughly chopped
	75 g (3 oz) stoned dates, chopped
	75 g (3 oz) seedless sultanas
	juice of 1 orange
	salt and pepper

TO GARNISH:
1 small bunch of coriander or basil, torn
orange wedges

Pour the stock into the bottom of a steamer and add the ground spices and bulgar wheat. Rinse the chicken breasts with cold water, drain them, then put them into the steamer top and sprinkle with the lemon and orange rind and a little salt and pepper.

Bring the stock to the boil, put the steamer top in place, cover with a lid and cook for 10 minutes until the chicken is thoroughly cooked and the bulgar wheat is tender. Remove the steamer top and cook the bulgar for a few further minutes if necessary.

Stir the dried fruits and orange juice into the bulgar, then spoon the bulgar and any stock on to 4 warmed plates. Slice the chicken pieces, arrange on top and garnish with torn herb leaves and orange wedges.

517 kcals (2170 kj) ■ **low fat** ■ **low GI** ■ **source of potassium** ■ **source of vitamins B and E**

137 Szechuan chicken

Preparation time:
10 minutes, plus
marinating

Cooking time:
15–20 minutes

Serves: 4

3 tablespoons soy sauce
2 tablespoons dry sherry
1 teaspoon rice vinegar
3 cm (1¼ inch) piece of fresh root ginger,
  peeled and finely chopped
1 garlic clove, crushed
1 tablespoon Chinese chilli paste
½ teaspoon Szechuan peppercorns,
  ground
1 tablespoon dark sesame oil
4 skinless chicken fillets, about 125 g
  (4 oz) each
coriander leaves, to garnish

TO SERVE:
cooked soba noodles
stir-fried oyster mushrooms

To make the marinade, mix together all the ingredients, except the chicken, in a shallow non-metallic dish. Add the chicken fillets, coat well, then cover and leave to marinate at room temperature for 2 hours.

Heat a griddle pan. Put the chicken on the griddle and cook for 7–10 minutes on each side. Garnish with coriander and serve with soba noodles and stir-fried oyster mushrooms.

NUTRITIONAL INFORMATION Ginger is a well known anti-nausea remedy and can also stimulate circulation and aid digestion. An infusion of grated ginger can help cold and bronchial symptoms.

237 kcals (991 kj) ■ **low fat** ■ **low carb** ■ **low GI** ■
source of potassium

138 Chicken satay sticks

Preparation time:
10 minutes, plus
marinating

Cooking time:
20 minutes

Serves: 4

4 skinless chicken fillets, about 125 g
  (4 oz) each
chopped coriander leaves, to garnish

MARINADE:
4 tablespoons soy sauce
4 tablespoons lime juice
1 garlic clove, crushed
1 teaspoon curry powder
1 teaspoon peanut butter
pinch of dried chilli flakes

SATAY SAUCE:
1 tablespoon peanut butter
2 tablespoons lime juice
1 teaspoon curry powder
1 garlic clove, crushed
4 tablespoons water

Put all the marinade ingredients into a shallow non-metallic dish and mix together until smooth.

Cut each chicken fillet lengthways into 3 strips. Thread the chicken pieces on to 12 presoaked bamboo skewers in an S-shape. Put into the marinade, coat well, cover and leave to marinate at room temperature for up to 2 hours.

To make the satay sauce, put all the ingredients into a small bowl and blend until smooth.

Heat a griddle pan. Put the chicken sticks, in batches, on the griddle and cook for 5 minutes on each side. Keep them warm in the oven while you cook the remainder. Serve the chicken sticks garnished with chopped coriander, and with the satay sauce for dipping.

231 kcals (964 kj) ■ **low fat** ■ **low carb** ■ **source of**
protein

139 Oriental chicken cakes

140 Tea-infused duck with flamed pak choi salad

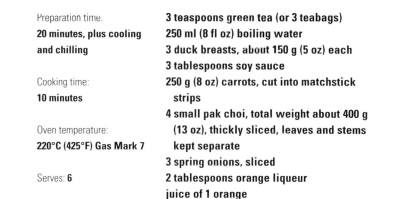

Preparation time:
15 minutes

Cooking time:
16 minutes

Serves: **4**

1 tablespoon sesame seeds
575 g (1 lb 3 oz) minced chicken
1 lemon grass stalk, finely chopped
2 kaffir lime leaves, finely chopped
5 cm (2 inch) piece of fresh root ginger,
**   peeled and finely chopped**
2 green chillies, finely chopped
2 garlic cloves, finely chopped
1 egg, beaten

TO SERVE:
cooked rice noodles
chopped peanuts
sliced onion
bean sprouts
chopped coriander
Chilli Jam (see recipe 130)

Toast the sesame seeds by dry-frying them in a frying pan until they begin to jump vigorously.

Put the minced chicken into a large bowl. Add the lemon grass, lime leaves, ginger, chilli and garlic; all these flavourings need to be so finely chopped that they almost make a paste. Add the beaten egg and toasted sesame seeds. Mix well, using your hands.

Heat a griddle pan. Divide the chicken mixture into 8 pieces. Using your hands, shape the pieces into small patties. Put the patties on the griddle and cook for 8 minutes on each side.

Serve the chicken cakes with a salad of rice noodles, chopped peanuts, sliced onion, bean sprouts and lots of chopped coriander, accompanied by Chilli Jam.

Preparation time:
20 minutes, plus cooling and chilling

Cooking time:
10 minutes

Oven temperature:
220°C (425°F) Gas Mark 7

Serves: **6**

3 teaspoons green tea (or 3 teabags)
250 ml (8 fl oz) boiling water
3 duck breasts, about 150 g (5 oz) each
3 tablespoons soy sauce
250 g (8 oz) carrots, cut into matchstick
**   strips**
4 small pak choi, total weight about 400 g
**   (13 oz), thickly sliced, leaves and stems**
**   kept separate**
3 spring onions, sliced
2 tablespoons orange liqueur
juice of 1 orange

Make the tea using the measurement boiling water, leave to infuse for 5 minutes, then strain and allow to cool.

Make crisscross cuts in the duck skin and put the duck, skin side up, into a shallow glass or china dish. Pour the tea over the duck breasts, cover with clingfilm and chill for 3–4 hours or overnight.

Put the duck breasts into a roasting tin, drizzle 1 tablespoon of the soy sauce over the skin and roast in a preheated oven, 220°C (425°F), Gas Mark 7, for 10 minutes until the skin is crisp but the meat is still slightly pink. After 5 minutes, pour 2 teaspoons fat from the roasting tin into a wok or frying pan.

Reheat the fat, add the carrot sticks and stir-fry for 2 minutes. Add the pak choi stems to the carrots and stir-fry for 1 minute. Add the pak choi leaves, spring onions and the remaining soy sauce and stir-fry for 30 seconds. Pour on the liqueur, set alight with a match and stand well back. When the flames subside, pour in the orange juice and warm through.

Spoon the vegetables into 6 small dishes and top with the drained and thinly sliced duck breast.

259 kcals (1083 kj) ▪ **low fat** ▪ **low carb** ▪ **low GI**

379 kcals (1564 kj) ▪ **low carb** ▪ **low GI** ▪ **source of iron**

141 Venison with root vegetables

142 Venison steaks with sesame and noodles

Preparation time: **15 minutes**	**400 g (13 oz) venison fillet, cut from the haunch**
	vegetable oil, for oiling
Cooking time: **about 45 minutes**	**4 small raw beetroots, peeled and sliced**
	2 pink sweet potatoes, peeled and sliced
	2 red onions
Oven temperature: **200°C (400°F) Gas Mark 6**	**100 g (3½ oz) redcurrant jelly**
	100 ml (3½ fl oz) red wine
	salt and pepper
Serves: **4**	**chopped parsley, to garnish**

Heat a griddle pan. Check that the venison fillet fits into the griddle pan; cut the fillet in half to fit if necessary. Cook the venison fillet on the griddle for 6 minutes on each side. Try to seal the outside evenly. Transfer the venison to a lightly oiled roasting tin and cook in a preheated oven, 200°C (400°F), Gas Mark 6, for a further 12–15 minutes for rare and up to 30 minutes for well done, depending on the thickness of the fillet.

Meanwhile, put the beetroot and sweet potato on the cleaned griddle and cook for 8–10 minutes on each side until soft. When cooked, add them to the venison in the oven.

Cut the onions into wedges, keeping the root ends intact to hold the wedges together. Griddle for 6 minutes on each side. Meanwhile, put the redcurrant jelly, wine and a little salt and pepper into a small saucepan and heat gently to melt the redcurrant jelly.

Remove the venison from the oven and allow to rest for a few minutes before carving. Add any meat juices to the redcurrant jelly sauce.

Arrange the griddled onions, beetroot and sweet potatoes on 4 warmed plates. Top with slices of venison, drizzle the sauce over the top and garnish with chopped parsley.

275 kcals (1150 kj) ▪ **low fat** ▪ **low GI** ▪ **source of antioxidants** ▪ **source of iron**

Preparation time: **10 minutes, plus marinating**	**4 lean venison steaks, about 150 g (5 oz) each**
	3 tablespoons soy sauce
	1 tablespoon oyster sauce
Cooking time: **about 5 minutes**	**1 tablespoon rice wine (mirin)**
	2 garlic cloves, crushed
	1 tablespoon finely grated fresh root ginger
Serves: **4**	**2 tablespoons groundnut oil**
	250 g (8 oz) spring greens or choi sum
	200 g (7 oz) buckwheat noodles
	1 tablespoon sesame oil

Put the venison steaks into a shallow bowl. Mix 2 tablespoons of the soy sauce with the oyster sauce, rice wine (mirin), garlic, ginger and groundnut oil, pour the marinade over the venison and coat thoroughly. Cover and leave to marinate in the refrigerator for 1–2 hours.

Put the spring greens or choi sum into a heatproof bowl and cover with boiling water. Leave for 1 minute, then drain well, reserving the vegetable water. Roughly chop the greens, set aside and keep warm.

Put the vegetable water into a large saucepan, add more water so that the pan is half full and bring to the boil. Add the noodles and return the water to the boil. Reduce the heat and simmer for 4–5 minutes, or until the noodles are just cooked but still firm.

Meanwhile, cook the venison steaks for 2 minutes on each side under a preheated grill or in a griddle pan, brushing them with any of the remaining marinade.

Drain the noodles as soon as they are cooked. Mix together the remaining soy sauce and the sesame oil and toss through the noodles. Cut the venison steaks into thick slices and serve immediately on a bed of noodles, topped with the wilted greens.

372 kcals (1555 kj) ▪ **low GI** ▪ **source of iron** ▪ **source of protein**

143 Rabbit with rosemary and mustard

144 Herby rabbit casserole

Preparation time:
10 minutes

Cooking time:
about 1 hour

Serves: **4**

1 teaspoon olive oil
1 onion, finely chopped
4 rabbit joints, about 200 g (7 oz) each
300 ml (½ pint) Chicken Stock (see Introduction)
200 ml (7 fl oz) dry white wine
2 teaspoons coarse-grain mustard
1 tablespoon chopped rosemary
3 tablespoons low-fat fromage frais
1 egg yolk
salt and pepper
rosemary sprigs, to garnish
steamed sugar snaps, to serve (optional)

Preparation time:
10 minutes

Cooking time:
45 minutes–1 hour
5 minutes

Serves: **4**

375 g (12 oz) lean rabbit, diced
1 tablespoon chopped rosemary, plus extra sprigs to garnish
1 tablespoon mixed herbs
1 tablespoon plain flour
1 teaspoon olive oil
1 red onion, cut into wedges
1 strip of orange rind
4 sun-dried tomatoes, rehydrated and chopped
150 ml (¼ pint) red wine
50 g (2 oz) Puy lentils, well rinsed
salt and pepper

Heat the oil in a large frying pan and gently fry the onion for 3 minutes. Add the rabbit joints and brown evenly on all sides. Add the stock, wine, mustard, rosemary and salt and pepper to taste. Cover the pan and simmer for 45 minutes until the rabbit is just tender.

Remove the rabbit joints to a serving dish and keep them warm. Boil the cooking liquid rapidly until reduced by half. Beat the fromage frais with the egg yolk and whisk into the cooking liquid over a gentle heat, without boiling. Spoon the sauce over the rabbit and garnish with rosemary sprigs. Serve with steamed sugar snaps, if liked.

Put the meat into a polythene bag with the rosemary, mixed herbs and flour. Toss the meat to coat, then remove.

Heat the oil in a saucepan and fry the meat until browned on all sides.

Add the onion, orange rind and tomatoes. Pour in the wine and add just enough water to cover the meat. Season well with salt and pepper. Cover the pan and simmer for 40 minutes–1 hour, or until the meat is tender and the vegetables are cooked.

Meanwhile, cook the lentils in a saucepan of boiling water for 20 minutes. Drain the lentils and add to the rabbit 10 minutes before the end of its cooking time. To serve, remove the orange rind and garnish with rosemary sprigs.

NUTRITIONAL INFORMATION Game provides all the important B vitamins, vital for the processing of food into energy.

336 kcals (1412 kj) ▪ low GI ▪ source of calcium ▪ source of vitamin B

236 kcals (990 kj) ▪ low fat ▪ low GI ▪ high fibre ▪ source of iron ▪ source of protein

145 Griddled turkey with citrus chilli sauce

Preparation time:
15 minutes

Cooking time:
15 minutes

Serves: **4**

grated rind and juice of 2 lemons
125 g (4 oz) sugar
1 onion, finely chopped
2 chillies, finely chopped
1 garlic clove, crushed
100 ml (3½ fl oz) water
4 turkey escalopes, about 175 g (6 oz)
  each
salt and pepper
basil leaves, torn, to garnish
steamed basmati rice, to serve

Put the lemon rind and juice, sugar, onion, chillies, garlic and the measurement water into a saucepan and simmer gently for 15 minutes. Watch this mixture carefully, as it will burn easily.

Meanwhile, heat a griddle pan. Season the escalopes to taste with salt and pepper, put on the griddle and cook for 5 minutes on each side.

Serve the escalopes on a bed of basmati rice with the chilli sauce poured over them, garnished with basil.

NUTRITIONAL INFORMATION Turkey is low in fat, provides high-quality protein and is a healthier alternative to minced beef when used in lasagne or burgers.

322 kcals (1350 kj) ▪ low fat ▪ low GI ▪ source of vitamin C

146 Roast guinea fowl with salsa verde

Preparation time:
30 minutes

Cooking time:
1 hour 5 minutes

Oven temperature:
190°C (375°F) Gas Mark 5

Serves: **6**

2 oven-ready guinea fowl, about 1 kg
  (2 lb) each
200 g (7 oz) extra fine green beans
75 g (3 oz) baby red Swiss chard leaves
pepper

SALSA VERDE:
50 g (2 oz) can anchovies in oil, drained
  and finely chopped
3 tablespoons chopped basil
3 tablespoons chopped parsley or chives
3 teaspoons capers, roughly chopped
2 teaspoons Dijon mustard
4 tablespoons olive oil
2 tablespoons white wine vinegar

First, to make the salsa verde, mix together all the ingredients in a bowl.

Rinse the guinea fowl with cold water and drain. Loosen the skin over each breast by inserting a small knife between the skin and flesh at the top of the breast. Remove the knife and slide a finger into the gap to enlarge the space, working down towards the other end of the breast. When you can reach no further, loosen the skin from the other end of the breast to meet in the middle. Do the same on the other bird.

Spoon a little of the salsa verde under the skin of both guinea fowl. Put the guinea fowl into a large roasting tin and cover loosely with foil. Roast in a preheated oven, 190°C (375°F), Gas Mark 5, for 1 hour 5 minutes, removing the foil for the last 10 minutes, until the juices run clear when you insert a skewer through the thickest part of the leg into the breast. Meanwhile, cook the green beans in boiling water for 5 minutes. Drain, return to the pan and toss with a little of the salsa verde and the Swiss chard. Spoon around the plate and serve with the sliced guinea fowl, drizzled with the remaining salsa verde.

550 kcals (2294 kj) ▪ low carb ▪ low GI ▪ source of antioxidants ▪ source of protein

147 Griddled duck with plum confit

Preparation time:
15 minutes

Cooking time:
1 hour

Oven temperature:
180°C (350°F) Gas Mark 4

Serves: **4**

450 g (14½ oz) new potatoes, scrubbed and thinly sliced
2 garlic cloves, thinly sliced
1 teaspoon chopped thyme
150 ml (¼ pint) water
2 tablespoons olive oil
4 boneless duck breasts, skinned
4 teaspoons Chinese five-spice powder
2 large onions, sliced
1 tablespoon sugar
2 tablespoons white wine vinegar
6 plums, halved, stoned and sliced
pepper
steamed green vegetables, to serve

Layer the potatoes with the garlic and thyme in a shallow ovenproof dish. Mix together the measurement water and half the oil and pour over the potatoes. Season well with pepper. Cover with foil and cook in a preheated oven, 180°C (350°F), Gas Mark 4, for 1 hour until the potatoes are tender, removing the foil halfway through cooking.

Meanwhile, rub the duck breasts with the five-spice powder. Cook the duck on a hot griddle or in a hot frying pan for 3–4 minutes on each side, pouring away any excess fat.

Heat the remaining oil in a small saucepan, add the onions and sugar and fry for 10 minutes until caramelized. Add the vinegar and plums, season to taste with pepper and cook for a further 10 minutes.

Slice the duck and serve with the potatoes and the plum confit, and plenty of green vegetables.

411 kcals (1724 kj) ▪ **low GI** ▪ **source of protein** ▪ **source of vitamin C**

148 Ostrich with mushrooms and spiced butter

Preparation time:
10 minutes

Cooking time:
15–25 minutes

Serves: **4**

4 large open-cap mushrooms, stalks removed
4 ostrich steaks or fillets, about 175 g (6 oz) each
flat leaf parsley, to garnish
roasted vine tomatoes, to serve (optional)

SPICED BUTTER·
2 shallots, finely chopped
2 garlic cloves, crushed
1 bunch of parsley, chopped
75 g (3 oz) butter, softened
1 teaspoon Worcestershire sauce
salt and pepper

Heat a griddle pan. Put the mushrooms, gill side down, on the griddle and cook for 5 minutes. Turn the mushrooms over and cook for a further 5 minutes. Keep the mushrooms warm in a low oven.

To make the spiced butter, mix together all the ingredients in a bowl.

Put the ostrich steaks on the griddle and cook for 3–4 minutes on each side for rare, 5 minutes for medium or 7 minutes for well done. To serve, arrange the mushrooms on 4 plates, add the griddled ostrich steaks and finally the spiced butter, divided between the 4 servings. Garnish with parsley and serve with roasted vine tomatoes, if liked.

COOK'S NOTES Ostrich meat tastes like slightly sweet beef and, because it is a very lean meat, is best served with a sauce, as here, to add a little moisture.

405 kcals (1693 kj) ▪ **low carb** ▪ **low GI** ▪ **source of antioxidants** ▪ **source of potassium**

7 Meat

149 Beef and mangetout stir-fry

150 Green beef curry

Preparation time:
10 minutes, plus
marinating

Cooking time:
5–8 minutes

Serves: **4**

**25 g (1 oz) fresh root ginger, peeled and
  shredded**
1 garlic clove, crushed
4 tablespoons light soy sauce
2 tablespoons dry sherry
1 teaspoon chilli sauce
1 teaspoon clear honey
½ teaspoon Chinese five-spice powder
375 g (12 oz) fillet steak, finely sliced
250 g (8 oz) dried egg noodles
250 g (8 oz) mangetout
salt and pepper
shredded spring onions, to garnish

Put the ginger, garlic, soy sauce, sherry, chilli sauce, honey and five-spice powder into a non-metallic bowl and stir well. Add the steak, stir to coat thoroughly, then cover and marinate in the refrigerator for at least 30 minutes.

Bring a large saucepan of lightly salted water to the boil. Add the noodles, then remove the pan from the heat, cover and allow to stand for 5 minutes.

Meanwhile, heat a wok or large frying pan. Add 2 tablespoons of the marinade and the beef and stir-fry for about 3–6 minutes. Add the mangetout and the remaining marinade, with salt and pepper if required, and stir-fry for a further 2 minutes.

Drain the noodles and arrange them in warmed serving bowls. Spoon the stir-fry over the top, garnish with shredded spring onions and serve.

Preparation time:
10 minutes

Cooking time:
10–15 minutes

Serves: **4**

300 g (10 oz) lean beef fillet, thinly sliced
1 red onion, cut into thin wedges
**125 g (4 oz) mangetout, thinly sliced
  lengthways**
150 ml (¼ pint) water
small handful of basil leaves
steamed basmati rice, to serve

THAI GREEN CURRY PASTE:
15 small green chillies
4 garlic cloves, halved
2 lemon grass stalks, finely chopped
2 lime leaves, torn
2 shallots, chopped
50 g (2 oz) coriander leaves and stalks
**2.5 cm (1 inch) piece of roughly chopped
  fresh root ginger**
2 teaspoons coriander seeds
1 teaspoon black peppercorns
1 teaspoon lemon rind
½ teaspoon salt
2 tablespoons groundnut oil.

Make the curry paste. Put all the ingredients into a food processor and whiz to a thick paste. Next, heat a nonstick wok and dry-fry the beef for 2 minutes. Remove with a slotted spoon, leaving the juices in the pan.

Reheat the pan and stir-fry the onion for 1 minute. Add 1–2 tablespoons of the curry paste, storing the remainder in a refrigerator for up to 3 weeks, and stir-fry for a further 1–2 minutes. Add the mangetout and measurement water, then return the meat to the pan and stir-fry for 5 minutes. When the beef is cooked, throw in the basil and stir-fry for 30 seconds. Serve with steamed basmati rice.

547 kcals (2295 kj) ■ **low GI** ■ **source of iron**

247 kcals (1036 kj) ■ **low carb** ■ **low GI** ■ **source of iron**

151 Hot and sour beef noodles

152 Thai beef salad

Preparation time:
20 minutes

Cooking time:
4–6 minutes, or to taste

Serves: **4**

1 tablespoon Szechuan peppercorns
400 g (13 oz) sirloin steak, about 1.5 cm
  (¾ inch) thick
1 cucumber, cut lengthways into strips
200 g (7 oz) dried rice vermicelli noodles,
  soaked in boiling water
1 red pepper, cored, deseeded and sliced
6 spring onions, finely sliced
500 g (1 lb) bean sprouts
1 bunch of mint, separated into leaves
1 tablespoon toasted sesame seeds

DRESSING:
50 ml (2 fl oz) lime juice
50 ml (2 fl oz) rice wine vinegar
2 lemon grass stalks, finely sliced
2 red chillies, deseeded and finely sliced
2 tablespoons Thai fish sauce
2 tablespoons dark brown sugar
2 tablespoons light soy sauce

Heat a griddle pan over a high heat. Crush the peppercorns and sprinkle on a plate, then press the steak firmly into the peppercorns. Put the steak on the griddle and cook for about 2–3 minutes on each side. Transfer it to a chopping board and allow to rest for a few minutes, then slice it thinly.

Mix together all the ingredients for the dressing. Mix 2 tablespoons with the cucumber strips. Toss the sliced steak with the noodles, pepper, spring onions, bean sprouts, mint leaves, sesame seeds and the remaining dressing. Divide between 4 warmed plates and scatter with the dressed cucumber strips.

Preparation time:
15 minutes, plus resting

Cooking time:
10–12 minutes

Serves: **4**

2 lean rump or sirloin steaks, about 150 g
  (5 oz) each, trimmed
150 g (5 oz) baby corn cobs
1 large cucumber
1 small red onion, finely chopped
3 tablespoons chopped coriander leaves
4 tablespoons rice wine vinegar
4 tablespoons sweet chilli dipping sauce
2 tablespoons lightly toasted sesame
  seeds, to garnish

Heat a griddle pan. Put the steaks on the griddle and cook for 3–4 minutes on each side. Allow to rest for 10–15 minutes, then slice them thinly.

Put the baby corn cobs into a saucepan of boiling water and cook for 3–4 minutes, or until tender. Refresh under cold running water and drain well.

Slice the cucumber in half lengthways, then scoop out and discard the seeds with a small spoon. Cut the cucumber into 5 mm (¼ inch) slices.

Put the steak, baby corn cobs, cucumber, onion and coriander into a large bowl. Stir in the vinegar and chilli sauce and mix well. Garnish the salad with sesame seeds and serve.

NUTRITIONAL INFORMATION Beef is an excellent source of iron, needed in haem, the molecule that carries oxygen in the blood. Good vegetarian sources include leafy green vegetables such as spinach and watercress, legumes and dried fruit such as apricots and figs.

608 kcals (2555 kj) ■ low GI ■ source of antioxidants ■ source of iron

278 kcals (1169 kj) ■ low carb ■ low GI ■ source of iron

153 Russian meatballs

154 Roast beef and tomatoes with mustard sauce

Preparation time:
15 minutes, plus chilling

Cooking time:
about 1 hour

Oven temperature:
180°C (350°F) Gas Mark 4

Serves: **4**

375 g (12 oz) lean minced beef
1 onion, roughly chopped
1 tablespoon tomato purée
1 teaspoon dried mixed herbs
salt and pepper
mashed potatoes, to serve (optional)

SAUCE:
1 red onion, finely chopped
400 g (13 oz) can chopped tomatoes
pinch of paprika
1 teaspoon dried mixed herbs

TO GARNISH:
parsley sprigs
chopped parsley
paprika

Put the minced beef, onion, tomato purée and herbs into a food processor or blender. Season well with salt and pepper, then whiz until smooth. Shape the mixture into 12 balls, cover and chill in the refrigerator for 30 minutes.

Meanwhile, put all the ingredients for the sauce into a saucepan and cook, uncovered, over a low heat for 15–20 minutes, stirring occasionally. Taste for seasoning. Pour the sauce into an ovenproof dish, arrange the meatballs on top and cook in a preheated oven, 180°C (350°F), Gas Mark 4, for 45 minutes.

Serve the meatballs sprinkled with chopped parsley and paprika and garnished with a parsley sprig. Accompany with mashed potatoes, if liked.

Preparation time:
20 minutes, plus resting

Cooking time:
30–45 minutes

Oven temperature:
220°C (425°F) Gas Mark 7

Serves: **8**

1.25 kg (2½ lb) fillet of beef
1 tablespoon olive oil, plus extra for oiling
1 garlic clove, sliced
2 red onions, sliced
16 small tomatoes
2 tablespoons Dijon mustard
2 tablespoons coarse-grain mustard
2 tablespoons clear honey
2 tablespoons chopped coriander leaves
salt and pepper

Heat a griddle pan. Season the fillet to taste with salt and pepper and pat in the seasoning. Put the fillet on the griddle and cook for 4 minutes on each side until charred on the outside.

Transfer the fillet to a lightly oiled roasting tin and cook in a preheated oven, 220°C (425°F), Gas Mark 7, for 10–15 minutes for rare and 20–25 minutes for medium. Remove from the oven and allow to rest for 10 minutes.

Heat the oil in a saucepan and fry the garlic and onions for 5 minutes. Add the tomatoes, season to taste with salt and pepper and warm through for 3 minutes.

Warm the 2 mustards in a small saucepan with the honey and stir until blended. Add the coriander leaves to the tomato mixture. Slice the fillet and serve on a bed of the tomato mixture, with the mustard sauce drizzled over it.

177 kcals (742 kj) ■ **low fat** ■ **low carb** ■ **low GI** ■ **source of iron**

482 kcals (2023 kj) ■ **low carb** ■ **low GI** ■ **source of antioxidants** ■ **source of iron**

155 Green peppercorn steak

Preparation time:
10 minutes

Cooking time:
about 10 minutes

Serves: **4**

4 lean fillet steaks, about 75 g (3 oz) each
1 tablespoon green peppercorns in brine, drained
2 tablespoons light soy sauce
1 teaspoon balsamic vinegar
8 cherry tomatoes, halved
thyme sprigs, to garnish
mashed potatoes, to serve (optional)

Heat a griddle pan until it is very hot. Put the steaks on the griddle and cook for 2–3 minutes on each side. Remove them from the griddle and keep warm.

Add the peppercorns, soy sauce, vinegar and tomatoes to the griddle pan and cook until the tomatoes are soft. Spoon the sauce over the steaks and garnish with thyme sprigs. Serve accompanied by mashed potatoes, if liked.

213 kcals (895 kj) ■ **low carb** ■ **low GI** ■ **source of antioxidants** ■ **source of iron**

156 Spiced beef fillet with haricot bean mash

Preparation time:
10 minutes

Cooking time:
about 15 minutes

Serves: **4**

1 teaspoon coriander seeds
1 teaspoon cumin seeds
1 teaspoon mixed peppercorns
4 fillet steaks, about 125 g (4 oz) each
1 teaspoon olive oil
2 x 400 g (13 oz) cans haricot beans, drained and rinsed
200 ml (7 fl oz) Vegetable Stock (see Introduction)
2 tablespoons low-fat crème fraîche
2 tablespoons chopped coriander leaves

Put the spices into a frying pan and dry-fry for 1 minute, then tip them into a mortar and roughly crush with a pestle.

Spread the spice mixture on a plate and press the steak into it so that it is covered all over. Heat the oil in the frying pan, add the steaks and cook for 3 minutes on each side, or until done to your liking. Remove them from the pan and keep warm.

Meanwhile, put the haricot beans and stock into a saucepan and bring to the boil. Reduce the heat and simmer for 10 minutes, then drain. Very lightly mash the beans with the crème fraîche and chopped coriander and serve with the steak.

574 kcals (2410 kj) ■ **low GI** ■ **high fibre** ■ **source of iron** ■ **source of protein**

157 One-pot beef

Preparation time:
25 minutes

Cooking time:
about 1½ hours

Oven temperature:
160°C (325°F) Gas Mark 3

Serves: **4–5**

**1 onion, sliced
750 g (1½ lb) topside of beef, trimmed
4 small baking potatoes, peeled and
  quartered
250 g (8 oz) baby carrots
250 g (8 oz) parsnips, cut into chunks
50 g (2 oz) pearl barley
2 bay leaves
900 ml (1½ pints) Beef or Chicken Stock
  (see Introduction)
1 tablespoon tomato purée
1 teaspoon coarse-grain mustard
150 g (5 oz) baby turnips
100 g (3½ oz) green beans
2 baby cabbages, quartered
salt and pepper
1 tablespoon cornflour mixed with a
  little water**

Put the onion into a flameproof casserole dish and stand the beef joint on top. Add the potatoes, carrots, parsnips, pearl barley and bay leaves. Pour the stock into the casserole and add the tomato purée, mustard and salt and pepper to taste. Bring to the boil, then cover the pan and transfer to a preheated oven, 160°C (325°F), Gas Mark 3, for 1¼ hours.

Lift the beef out of the casserole, put it on a plate and wrap it in foil to keep warm. Add the turnips to the casserole, cover the pan and simmer on the hob for 5 minutes. Add the green vegetables and cook for a further 5–8 minutes until just tender and still bright green. Stir in the cornflour mixture and cook for 1 minute.

Thinly slice the beef and arrange on warmed plates. Lift the vegetables out of the pan with a slotted spoon and arrange them around the beef. Spoon the gravy, onions and pearl barley over the meat.

370 kcals (1560 kj) ■ **low fat** ■ **high fibre** ■ **source of iron** ■ **source of protein**

158 Griddled provençal beef

Preparation time:
15 minutes

Cooking time:
10–20 minutes

Serves: **4**

**575 g (1 lb 3 oz) thick sirloin steak
100 g (3½ oz) thin green beans
4 beef tomatoes, skinned
1 bunch of flat leaf parsley, chopped
425 g (14 oz) can butter beans, drained
  and rinsed
100 g (3½ oz) pitted black olives
salt**

DRESSING:
**2 tablespoons Dijon mustard
6 tablespoons olive oil
2 tablespoons wine vinegar
salt and pepper**

Heat a griddle pan. Put the steak on the griddle and cook for 5 minutes on each side for rare, 8 minutes for medium or 10 minutes for well-done meat.

Meanwhile, cook the green beans in a saucepan of lightly salted boiling water for 3 minutes, then refresh under cold running water. Drain them well.

Cut the tomatoes into wedges and remove and discard the cores and seeds. Combine the tomatoes, green beans, parsley, butter beans and olives and arrange in a serving dish.

To make the dressing, mix together all the ingredients in a small jug. Remove the steak from the griddle and allow to rest for 5 minutes, then carve into thin slices. Arrange the pieces overlapping each other slightly on top of the salad and drizzle with the dressing.

760 kcals (3191 kj) ■ **low GI** ■ **high fibre** ■ **source of antioxidants** ■ **source of iron**

159 Veal escalopes with parsley pesto

160 Ratatouille lamb pie

Preparation time:
15 minutes

Cooking time:
10 minutes

Serves: **4**

**4 veal escalopes, about 150 g (5 oz) each
cooked penne, to serve (optional)**

PARSLEY PESTO:
**100 g (3½ oz) pine nuts
1 large bunch of parsley, plus extra to
 garnish
4 tablespoons olive oil
2 garlic cloves, crushed
grated rind of 2 lemons, plus extra to
 garnish
4 tablespoons lemon juice
salt and pepper**

To make the pesto, heat a dry frying pan until hot, add the pine nuts and toast lightly, shaking the pan frequently. Transfer to a food processor or blender with all the remaining ingredients and whiz until smooth.

Heat a griddle pan. Put the veal escalopes on the griddle and cook for 5 minutes on each side. Serve the veal with spoonfuls of the parsley pesto to the side or on top, garnished with extra lemon rind and parsley sprigs, and accompanied by penne, if liked.

Preparation time:
20 minutes

Cooking time:
45–50 minutes

Oven temperature:
200°C (400°F) Gas Mark 6

Serves: **4**

**500 g (1 lb) lean lamb fillet, trimmed and
 roughly chopped
3 tablespoons olive oil
1 small aubergine, about 300 g (10 oz),
 diced
2 onions, chopped
2 garlic cloves, crushed
400 g (13 oz) can chopped tomatoes
2 tablespoons sun-dried tomato paste
2 red peppers, cored, deseeded and
 roughly chopped
2 courgettes, sliced
1 tablespoon chopped thyme
3 sheets of filo pastry, about 150 g (5 oz)
2 teaspoons sesame seeds
salt and pepper
thyme sprigs, to garnish**

Whiz the lamb in a food processor until it is chopped into small pieces. Heat 2 tablespoons of the oil in a large frying pan, add the lamb, aubergine and onions and fry, stirring, for 5–10 minutes until browned.

Add the garlic, tomatoes, tomato paste, peppers, courgettes, thyme and a little salt and pepper and bring just to the boil. Reduce the heat, cover the pan and cook gently for 20 minutes until the lamb is tender and the sauce is pulpy. Turn into a shallow 1.8 litre (3 pint) pie dish.

Crumple one filo sheet to the dimensions of the pie dish and brush with a little oil. Crumple another sheet over this one and brush with more oil. Crumple the final filo sheet on top. Carefully lift the pastry over the filling, easing it to fit so that the edges just cover the rim of the dish. Brush the filo with any remaining oil and scatter with sesame seeds. Bake in a preheated oven, 200°C (400°F), Gas Mark 6, for about 20 minutes until the pastry is golden. Serve garnished with thyme.

480 kcals (2017 kj) ■ **low carb** ■ **low GI** ■ **high fibre** ■ **source of iron** ■ **source of vitamin C**

526 kcals (2207 kj) ■ **low GI** ■ **source of antioxidants** ■ **source of iron**

161 Griddled Italian lamb with rosemary oil

162 Moroccan lamb

Preparation time:
10 minutes

Cooking time:
20–40 minutes

Serves: **4**

2 lamb fillets, about 750 g (1½ lb), trimmed
4 garlic cloves, cut into slivers
few small rosemary sprigs
2 red onions, quartered
4 tablespoons olive oil
1 tablespoon chopped rosemary
salt and pepper

TO SERVE:
cooked fresh linguine, lightly tossed in
** olive oil**
Parmesan cheese shavings

Preparation time:
10 minutes

Cooking time:
1 hour

Serves: **4**

1 kg (2 lb) boned leg of lamb
2 garlic cloves, crushed
1 teaspoon paprika
1 teaspoon ground cumin
1 teaspoon ground coriander
1 teaspoon ground ginger
1 teaspoon ground cinnamon
good pinch of dried chilli flakes
coriander sprigs, to garnish

TO SERVE:
harissa
Moroccan Griddled Vegetable Salad (see
** recipe 73), optional**

Heat a griddle pan. Make small incisions all over the fillets and insert the garlic slivers and rosemary sprigs. Put the fillets on the griddle and cook, turning occasionally until charred all over, for about 20 minutes for rare or 30–40 minutes for well done. Add the onions for the last 10 minutes and char on the outside. Allow the lamb to rest for 5 minutes, then carve into slices.

Meanwhile, put the oil and rosemary into a mortar and crush with a pestle to release the flavours. Season to taste with salt and pepper. Spoon the rosemary oil over the lamb slices and serve immediately with the griddled onions, cooked fresh linguine lightly tossed in olive oil, and Parmesan shavings.

Trim the lamb of excess fat. Mix the crushed garlic with the spices and rub the mixture all over the lamb, covering it well.

Heat a griddle pan. Put the lamb on the griddle and cook for 30 minutes on each side. Begin with the griddle very hot so as to seal the meat, then reduce the heat so that the outside of the meat does not become too blackened.

Remove the lamb from the griddle and allow to rest for 5 minutes before carving. Garnish with coriander sprigs and serve with harissa and Moroccan Griddled Vegetable Salad, if liked.

NUTRITIONAL INFORMATION The medicinal uses of rosemary include memory enhancement and the stimulation of blood circulation. It can also help to alleviate headaches and migraine.

487 kcals (2036 kj) ▪ low carb ▪ source of antioxidants
▪ source of iron

NUTRITIONAL INFORMATION Meat is a good source of zinc, iron and some of the B vitamins, but it is best to choose lean cuts that are lower in saturated fat.

298 kcals (1246 kj) ▪ low fat ▪ low carb ▪ source of iron

163 Spinach-stuffed lamb

164 Lamb steaks with green and cannellini beans

Preparation time:
20 minutes

Cooking time:
45–55 minutes

Oven temperature:
180°C (350°F) Gas Mark 4

Serves: **4**

250 g (8 oz) spinach, cooked, drained and chopped
15 g (½ oz) mint, finely chopped
4 garlic cloves, finely chopped
1 teaspoon vinegar
pinch of sugar
½ small leg of lamb (knuckle end), boned
175 ml (6 fl oz) red wine
salt and pepper

TO SERVE:
salad leaves (optional)
shredded carrot (optional)

Preparation time:
20 minutes

Cooking time:
25 minutes

Serves: **4**

4 lean lamb leg steaks, about 150 g (5 oz) each
2 tablespoons olive oil, plus extra for brushing
2 onions, chopped
2 garlic cloves, crushed
425 g (14 oz) can cannellini beans, drained and rinsed
1 tablespoon molasses
400 g (13 oz) can chopped tomatoes
2 tablespoons tomato purée
150 g (5 oz) green beans
125 g (4 oz) spinach
salt and pepper
coriander leaves, to garnish

Mix together the spinach, mint, garlic, vinegar, sugar and salt and pepper to taste in a bowl.

Trim every scrap of fat from the lamb. Lay it flat with the boned side up and spread over the spinach mixture. Fold over the meat and secure with string as if tying a parcel. Put the meat into a roasting dish or tin and pour over the wine, adding a little water if the tin is much larger than the meat. Cook in a preheated oven, 180°C (350°F), Gas Mark 4, for 45–55 minutes, depending on how well done you like lamb.

Transfer the lamb to a hot platter and carve into thick slices. Pour off the excess fat from the roasting tin and pour the remaining juices around the lamb slices. Serve immediately with salad leaves and shredded carrot, if liked.

Season the lamb steaks to taste with salt and pepper. Heat the oil in a saucepan and fry the onions until soft and golden brown. Add the garlic and cook for a further 1 minute. Add the canned beans to the pan with the molasses, tomatoes and tomato purée and bring to a fast simmer.

Put the green beans into a steamer over the simmering beans. Reduce the heat slightly, cover the steamer with a lid and cook for 15 minutes. Add a little water to the beans if they begin to dry out.

Meanwhile, heat a griddle pan. Lightly brush the lamb steaks with oil, put on the griddle and cook for 4–5 minutes on each side for medium or 6–8 minutes for well done.

Add the spinach to the beans in the tomato sauce. Stir well and season to taste with salt and pepper.

Serve the lamb steaks on a bed of cannellini beans and spinach, and top with the steamed green beans. Garnish with coriander leaves.

190 kcals (794 kj) ▪ **low fat** ▪ **low carb** ▪ **low GI** ▪ **source of iron**

429 kcals (1793 kj) ▪ **low GI** ▪ **high fibre** ▪ **source of iron** ▪ **source of vitamin C**

165 Roast pork fillet with rosemary and fennel

166 Pork fillet with apricots

Preparation time:
10 minutes

Cooking time:
about 30 minutes

Oven temperature:
230°C (450°F) Gas Mark 8

Serves: **4**

2 teaspoons olive oil
1 large rosemary sprig, broken into small
  pieces
3 garlic cloves, sliced
750 g (1 lb) pork fillet, trimmed
2 fennel bulbs, trimmed, cored and cut
  into wedges
150 ml (¼ pint) white wine
75 g (3 oz) quark cheese
salt and pepper
rosemary sprigs, to garnish

Heat half the oil in a nonstick frying pan and gently fry the rosemary and garlic for 1–2 minutes. Add the pork fillet and fry for 5 minutes, or until it is browned all over. Remove the pork from the frying pan (don't clean the pan, although you may wish to remove the bits of rosemary and garlic with a slotted spoon).

Put the fennel wedges into a nonstick roasting tin and drizzle with the remaining oil. Put the pork fillet on top and season generously with salt and pepper. Transfer to a preheated oven, 230°C (450°F), Gas Mark 8, and roast for 20 minutes.

Meanwhile, pour the wine into the frying pan and simmer until it has reduced by half, scraping any bits of pork fillet into the wine. Add the quark and season to taste with salt and pepper. Stir well to mix.

To serve, slice the pork and arrange on a warmed serving dish with the fennel. Pour the sauce into the roasting tin and cook briefly over a medium heat, stirring well. Spoon the sauce over the pork and fennel, garnish with rosemary sprigs and serve immediately.

Preparation time:
10 minutes

Cooking time:
about 35 minutes

Serves: **4**

700 g (1 lb 7 oz) pork fillet, sliced into
  2.5 cm (1 inch) rounds
2 red onions
8 apricots, halved and stoned
1 bunch of thyme
4 tablespoons olive oil
1 tablespoon cider vinegar
salt and pepper
spiced rice, to serve

Heat a griddle pan. Put the pork rounds on the griddle and cook for 7–8 minutes on each side, then place in an ovenproof dish and transfer to a warm oven.

Cut the onions into wedges, keeping the root ends intact to hold the wedges together. Put on the griddle and cook for 5 minutes on each side. Add to the pork in the oven.

Put the apricot halves on the griddle and cook for 5 minutes on each side. Add the thyme for the last minute of cooking, then transfer everything to the oven.

Mix together the oil, vinegar and a little salt and pepper and drizzle over the griddled meat and vegetables. Serve with spiced rice.

296 kcals (1237 kj) ■ **low fat** ■ **low carb** ■ **low GI** ■
source of calcium

445 kcals (1860 kj) ■ **low carb** ■ **low GI** ■ **source of**
antioxidants ■ **source of potassium**

Preparation time:
15 minutes

Cooking time:
35 minutes

Oven temperature:
200°C (400°F) Gas Mark 6

Serves: **4**

2 yellow peppers, cored, deseeded and quartered
2 red peppers, cored, deseeded and quartered
2 courgettes, sliced
2 red onions
1 bunch of sage, roughly chopped, plus extra to garnish
4 pork steaks, 150 g (5 oz) each
1 garlic clove, halved
dash of white wine
salt and pepper

Heat a griddle pan. Put the peppers on the griddle and cook for 6 minutes on the skin side and 3 minutes on the other. Transfer them to a large ovenproof dish and put into a preheated oven, 200°C (400°F), Gas Mark 6.

Griddle the courgette slices for 2 minutes on each side. Remove from the griddle and add to the dish of peppers.

Cut the onions into wedges, keeping the root ends intact to hold the wedges together. Cook on the griddle for 4 minutes on each side. Add half the sage to the onions for the last minute of cooking. Mix the griddled sage and onions with the other vegetables in the oven.

Rub the pork steaks all over with the halved garlic clove and griddle them for 6 minutes on each side. Add to the vegetables in the oven.

Finally, add the remaining sage, wine and a little salt and pepper to the griddle pan. Bring to the boil.

To serve, arrange the griddled vegetables on warmed individual plates and top with the pork. Drizzle over the wine and sage sauce and garnish with sage leaves.

Preparation time:
20 minutes

Cooking time:
25 minutes

Serves: **4**

575 g (1 lb 3 oz) lean minced pork
3.5 cm (1½ inch) piece of galangal, peeled and finely chopped
4 garlic cloves, finely chopped
1 bunch of coriander, finely chopped
1 lemon grass stalk, finely chopped
2 chillies, finely chopped
1 tablespoon Thai fish sauce
1 egg, beaten

TO GARNISH:
griddled chillies
griddled lemon grass

Put the minced pork into a bowl. Add all the remaining ingredients and mix well.

Heat a griddle pan. Divide the pork mixture into 12 pieces. Using your hands, shape the pieces into balls, then flatten them slightly. If the mixture sticks to your hands, try dipping your hands in cold water before forming the pork cakes.

Put the pork cakes, in batches, on the griddle and cook for 6 minutes on each side. Keep them warm in the oven while you cook the remainder. To serve, pile the pork cakes on a warmed serving dish and garnish with griddled chillies and lemon grass.

COOK'S NOTES Galangal is widely used in Far Eastern cookery. **Found in fresh, dried or ground form, it is similar to ginger in flavour and appearance. In Indonesia it is known as laos and kenkur, and is sometimes found in specialist shops under the name of laos powder.**

147 kcals (614 kj) ▪ **low fat** ▪ **low carb** ▪ **low GI** ▪ **source of antioxidants** ▪ **source of vitamin C**

203 kcals (849 kj) ▪ **low fat** ▪ **low carb**

169 Lentils with broad beans, bacon and egg

170 Tagliatelle with bacon, mushroom and pine nuts

Preparation time:
15 minutes

Cooking time:
30 minutes

Serves: **2**

75 g (3 oz) Puy lentils, well rinsed
1 thyme sprig
1 celery stick, roughly chopped
1 garlic clove
1 litre (1¾ pints) water
1 tablespoon olive oil
3 rashers of smoked back bacon, roughly chopped
4 spring onions, finely sliced
200 g (7 oz) frozen broad beans, blanched and outer skins removed
1 tablespoon balsamic vinegar
2 eggs
salt and pepper

Preparation time:
10 minutes

Cooking time:
10–12 minutes

Serves: **4**

375 g (12 oz) green and white dried tagliatelle
1 tablespoon olive oil
1 yellow pepper, cored, deseeded and chopped
2 teaspoons garlic purée or crushed garlic
125 g (4 oz) button mushrooms, sliced
125 g (4 oz) rindless lean back bacon, grilled and cut into thin strips
1 tablespoon chopped parsley
500 g (1 lb) fromage frais or low-fat natural yogurt
25 g (1 oz) pine nuts
pepper

Put the lentils, thyme, celery and garlic into a saucepan and pour over the measurement water. Bring to the boil, then reduce the heat and simmer for 20 minutes until tender. Drain the lentils and discard the thyme, celery and garlic.

Heat the oil and fry the bacon for 2–3 minutes, then add the spring onions and broad beans and fry for a further 2–3 minutes. Add the lentils and continue to cook for 1 minute. Season to taste with salt and pepper and stir in the vinegar.

Meanwhile, poach the eggs in simmering water for 2 minutes. Remove with a slotted spoon and drain on kitchen paper. Divide the lentil mixture between 2 plates and top each mound with a poached egg. Serve immediately.

Cook the tagliatelle in a large saucepan of boiling water for 10–12 minutes, or according to the packet instructions, until al dente.

Meanwhile, heat the oil in a nonstick frying pan, add the pepper and cook for 2–3 minutes. Stir in the garlic, mushrooms, bacon, parsley and pepper to taste. Reduce the heat and stir in the fromage frais or yogurt. Heat through very gently.

Heat a dry frying pan until hot, add the pine nuts and toast lightly, shaking the pan frequently.

Drain the pasta and toss with the sauce. Sprinkle with the toasted pine nuts before serving.

447 kcals (1869 kj) ■ **high fibre** ■ **source of phytoestrogens** ■ **source of protein**

577 kcals (2412 kj) ■ **low GI** ■ **source of protein**

171 Prosciutto and pear sticks

172 Tagliatelle romana

Preparation time: **10 minutes**	**6 slices of prosciutto** **2 ripe pears** **olive oil, for oiling and drizzling**
Cooking time: **4–6 minutes**	**pepper**
Serves: **4**	TO SERVE: **salad leaves** **Parmesan cheese shavings**

Cut each slice of prosciutto in half lengthways. Cut each pear into 6 wedges and remove the cores.

Wrap a piece of prosciutto around each pear wedge and thread 3 wedges on to a skewer.

Put the skewers on an oiled grill rack and cook under a preheated hot grill for 2–3 minutes on each side. Serve immediately on a bed of salad leaves, sprinkled with Parmesan shavings and pepper and drizzled with a little oil.

Preparation time: **10 minutes**	**1.5 litres (2½ pints) Chicken Stock (see Introduction)** **250 g (8 oz) dried tagliatelle**
Cooking time: **10–12 minutes**	**125 g (4 oz) quark cheese** **1 garlic clove, crushed** **50 g (2 oz) smoked prosciutto, fat**
Serves: **4**	**removed, cut into strips** **salt and pepper** **thyme leaves, to garnish**

Pour the stock into a large saucepan and bring to the boil. Add the tagliatelle, stir and cook for 10–12 minutes, or according to the packet instructions, until al dente. Drain and turn into a warmed serving dish.

Sieve the quark, mix in the garlic and season to taste with salt and pepper. Stir the cheese mixture into the tagliatelle and toss in the prosciutto strips. Garnish with thyme leaves and serve immediately.

126 kcals (527 kj) ■ **low fat** ■ **low carb** ■ **high fibre** ■ **source of vitamin C**

314 kcals (1313 kj) ■ **low fat** ■ **low GI** ■ **source of calcium**

8 Vegetarian

173 Vegetable pancakes with ginger sauce

Preparation time:	8 ready-made rice pancakes
15 minutes	2 carrots
	100 g (3½ oz) bean sprouts
Cooking time:	small handful of mint, roughly chopped
about 5 minutes	1 celery stick, thinly sliced
	4 spring onions, thinly sliced diagonally
Serves: **4**	1 tablespoon soy sauce

SAUCE:
1 garlic clove, roughly chopped
5 cm (2 inch) piece of fresh root ginger, peeled and roughly chopped
3 tablespoons light muscovado sugar
4 teaspoons soy sauce
5 teaspoons wine or rice vinegar
2 tablespoons tomato purée
2 tablespoons sesame seeds, plus extra to garnish

Put all the ingredients for the sauce, except the sesame seeds, into a food processor or blender and whiz to a thin paste. Stir in the sesame seeds and transfer to a serving bowl.

Soften the rice pancakes according to the packet instructions. Cut the carrots into fine shreds and mix them with the bean sprouts, mint, celery, spring onions and soy sauce.

Divide the vegetable mixture between the 8 pancakes and spoon into the middle of each one. Fold the bottom edge of each pancake to the middle, then roll it up from one side to the other to form a pocket.

Steam the pancakes in a steamer for about 5 minutes until warmed. Serve immediately with the sauce, garnished with sesame seeds.

156 kcals (654 kj) ■ **low fat** ■ **source of magnesium** ■ **source of vitamin C**

174 Baby squash with red bean sauce

Preparation time:	600 ml (1 pint) Vegetable Stock (see Introduction)
10 minutes	1 kg (2 lb) mixed baby squash
Cooking time:	125 g (4 oz) baby spinach
15–20 minutes	steamed basmati rice, to serve
Serves: **4**	

RED BEAN SAUCE:
3 tablespoons olive oil
4 garlic cloves, thinly sliced
1 red pepper, cored, deseeded and finely chopped
2 tomatoes, chopped
400 g (13 oz) can red kidney beans, drained and rinsed
1–2 tablespoons hot chilli sauce
small handful of coriander, chopped
salt

Bring the stock to the boil in a large saucepan. Quarter and deseed the squash, then add them to the pan. Reduce the heat, cover the pan and simmer gently for about 15 minutes, or until the squash are just tender.

Meanwhile, to make the sauce, heat the oil in a frying pan and fry the garlic and pepper for 5 minutes, stirring frequently, until very soft. Add the tomatoes, kidney beans, chilli sauce and a little salt and simmer for 5 minutes until the mixture is pulpy.

Remove the squash from the stock with a slotted spoon. Pour the stock into a bowl and reserve. Return the squash to the pan, add the spinach, then cover and cook for about 1 minute until the spinach has wilted.

Divide the steamed rice between 4 serving plates and pile the vegetables on top. Stir 8 tablespoons of the reserved stock into the sauce with the chopped coriander and pour over the vegetables.

256 kcals (1074 kj) ■ **low fat** ■ **source of antioxidants**

175 Sweet and sour vegetables

Preparation time:
15 minutes

Cooking time:
5 minutes

Serves: **4**

2 tablespoons groundnut oil
3 garlic cloves, chopped
1 cucumber, halved, deseeded and
 diagonally chopped into 5 mm (¼ inch)
 slices
4 baby corn cobs, diagonally sliced
1 tomato, cut into 8 pieces
250 g (8 oz) can water chestnuts, drained
50 g (2 oz) mangetout
1 onion, roughly chopped
4 tablespoons Vegetable Stock (see
 Introduction)
1 tablespoon sugar
1 tablespoon soy sauce
1 tablespoon distilled white vinegar or
 Chinese rice vinegar
3 spring onions, roughly chopped
salt and pepper

Heat the oil in a wok or heavy-based frying pan and quickly stir-fry the garlic. When the garlic is turning golden, add all the remaining ingredients, except the spring onions, and cook, stirring constantly, for 2–3 minutes. Add salt and pepper to taste, then add the spring onions and cook for 30 seconds. Serve immediately.

138 kcals (581 kj) ■ **low fat** ■ **low carb** ■ **low GI**

176 Thai sesame and tofu stir-fry

Preparation time:
15 minutes

Cooking time:
about 10 minutes

Serves: **4**

1 teaspoon sesame oil
2 tablespoons teriyaki sauce
400 g (13 oz) firm tofu, cut into 4 slices
2 tablespoons sesame seeds
1 tablespoon rice wine vinegar or dry
 sherry
2 teaspoons soy sauce
1 tablespoon groundnut oil
16 mangetout
1 carrot, cut into thin strips
125 g (4 oz) bean sprouts
2 spring onions, white parts cut into 5 cm
 (2 inch) batons, green tops shredded
 to garnish
250 g (8 oz) dried rice noodles, prepared
 according to the packet instructions
50 g (2 oz) watercress, broken into sprigs

Mix together the sesame oil and half the teriyaki sauce in a small bowl. Brush over both sides of the tofu. Sprinkle one side of each piece of tofu with half the sesame seeds. Mix together the remaining teriyaki sauce, vinegar or sherry and soy sauce. Set aside.

Heat a wok and brush with a little groundnut oil. Cook the tofu, seeded side down, for 2 minutes. Sprinkle the remaining sesame seeds over the tofu, then turn it and cook for a further 2 minutes until crisp. Remove from the pan and keep warm. Brush the wok with more groundnut oil, then add the mangetout, carrot, bean sprouts and spring onion batons. Stir-fry for 2–3 minutes until tender yet crisp. Add the reserved teriyaki sauce mixture and stir-fry for 1 minute.

Divide the hot noodles between 4 warmed serving bowls. Add the watercress, then the vegetable mixture and top with the tofu. Garnish with the shredded spring onion.

440 kcals (1849 kj) ■ **low GI** ■ **source of protein** ■ **source of vitamin B**

177 Thai vegetable curry

178 Pumpkin curry

Preparation time:
10–15 minutes

Cooking time:
30–35 minutes

Serves: **4**

2 tablespoons sunflower oil
1 onion, chopped
2 garlic cloves, crushed
5 cm (2 inch) piece of fresh root ginger,
  peeled and grated
1½ tablespoons Thai red curry paste
600 ml (1 pint) Vegetable Stock (see
  Introduction)
3 kaffir lime leaves
250 g (8 oz) sweet potatoes, peeled and
  diced
250 g (8 oz) pumpkin, peeled, deseeded
  and cubed
8 baby corn cobs
1 aubergine, roughly chopped
125 g (4 oz) green beans, chopped
125 g (4 oz) small button mushrooms
200 g (7 oz) can bamboo shoots, drained
salt and pepper
boiled jasmine rice, to serve

Heat the oil in large saucepan and gently fry the onion, garlic and ginger for 5 minutes, stirring occasionally. Stir in the curry paste and fry gently for 3 minutes, stirring constantly.

Add the stock and lime leaves and bring to the boil, then add salt and pepper to taste. Reduce the heat and simmer for 2 minutes. Add the sweet potatoes and pumpkin, cover the pan and simmer for 10 minutes. Add the baby corn cobs, aubergine, green beans, mushrooms and bamboo shoots, replace the lid and simmer for a further 5–10 minutes, or until the beans are just tender but still crisp.

Taste and adjust the seasoning if necessary. Serve the curry with jasmine rice.

193 kcals (809 kj) ■ **low fat** ■ **source of antioxidants**

Preparation time:
20 minutes, plus soaking

Cooking time:
30–35 minutes

Serves: **6**

50 g (2 oz) fresh coconut, grated
300 ml (½ pint) coconut water (from a
  fresh coconut)
2 tablespoons vegetable oil
1 onion, chopped
1 green pepper, cored, deseeded and
  chopped
4 garlic cloves, crushed
2 slices of fresh root ginger, peeled and
  finely chopped
¼ teaspoon turmeric
2 fresh green chillies, deseeded and
  finely chopped
¼ teaspoon ground cloves
¼ teaspoon crushed chilli flakes
750 g (1½ lb) pumpkin, peeled, deseeded
  and cut into 2.5 cm (1 inch) cubes
2 tomatoes, skinned and chopped
salt and pepper

Put the coconut into a bowl and add the coconut water. You can drain this out of a fresh coconut by piercing it twice with a skewer and pouring out the liquid. (If you don't get enough liquid, make up the quantity with water.) Leave the coconut to soak for about 30 minutes.

Heat the oil in a saucepan and gently fry the onion, pepper and garlic over a very low heat, stirring occasionally, until the onion and pepper are softened and golden brown. Add the ginger, turmeric, chillies, cloves and chilli flakes and cook, stirring, for a further 2–3 minutes.

Add the pumpkin, tomatoes, coconut and coconut water. Bring to the boil, then reduce the heat to a bare simmer. Cover the pan and cook for 20 minutes, or until the pumpkin is tender but not mushy. Season to taste with salt and pepper and serve.

109 kcals (459 kj) ■ **low fat** ■ **low carb** ■ **source of antioxidants**

179 Curried tofu burgers

180 Tofu with pak choi and shiitake mushrooms

Preparation time: **15 minutes**	**2 tablespoons vegetable oil** **1 large carrot, coarsely grated** **1 small red onion, finely chopped**
Cooking time: **10–15 minutes**	**1 garlic clove, crushed** **1 teaspoon hot curry paste** **1 teaspoon sun-dried tomato paste**
Serves: **4**	**250 g (8 oz) firm tofu, drained** **25 g (1 oz) wholemeal breadcrumbs** **25 g (1 oz) unsalted peanuts, finely chopped** **plain flour, for dusting** **salt and pepper**

TO SERVE:
burger bun
fried onion rings
green salad leaves
alfalfa

Heat half the oil in a large nonstick frying pan and fry the carrot and onion, stirring constantly, for 3–4 minutes, or until the vegetables are softened. Add the garlic and curry and tomato pastes. Increase the heat and fry for 2 minutes, stirring constantly.

Whiz the tofu, vegetables, breadcrumbs and nuts in a food processor or blender until just combined. Transfer to a bowl, season well with salt and pepper and beat until the mixture starts to stick together.

Shape the mixture into 4 burgers. Heat the remaining oil in a large nonstick frying pan and fry the burgers for 3–4 minutes on each side, or until golden brown. Alternatively, to grill the burgers, brush them with a little oil and cook under a preheated hot grill for about 3 minutes on each side, or until golden brown. Drain on kitchen paper and serve in a burger bun, garnished with fried onion rings, salad leaves and alfalfa.

Preparation time: **15 minutes**	**3 teaspoons vegetable oil** **200 g (7 oz) firm tofu, drained and cut into 2.5 cm (1 inch) cubes**
Cooking time: **about 10 minutes**	**1 garlic clove, crushed** **150 g (5 oz) shiitake mushrooms, roughly chopped**
Serves: **2**	**200 g (7 oz) pak choi, roughly chopped** **4 spring onions, finely sliced** **2 tablespoons plum sauce** **2 tablespoons light soy sauce** **2 tablespoons water** **125 g (4 oz) dried rice noodles**

Heat half the oil in a wok or frying pan and stir-fry the tofu for 2–3 minutes, or until golden brown. Remove with a slotted spoon and set aside.

Heat the remaining oil in the pan and stir-fry the garlic, mushrooms, pak choi and spring onions for 2–3 minutes. Stir in the tofu, plum sauce, soy sauce and measurement water and cook for a further 2 minutes, or until the sauce is hot.

Prepare the noodles according to the packet instructions. Divide them between 2 bowls, spoon over the tofu mixture and serve immediately.

NUTRITIONAL INFORMATION Tofu (soya bean curd) is rich in protein and B vitamins, low in saturated fat and sodium and an important non-dairy source of calcium. Soya protein has been shown to decrease total and LDL cholesterol.

120 kcals (503 kj) ■ **low fat** ■ **low carb** ■ **source of protein** ■ **source of vitamin B**

405 kcals (1690 kj) ■ **low fat** ■ **source of calcium** ■ **source of protein** ■ **source of vitamin B**

181 Rigatoni with tomatoes and chilli

182 Linguine with courgette and gremolata

Preparation time:
10 minutes

Cooking time:
10–12 minutes

Serves: **4**

300 g (10 oz) dried rigatoni
2 tablespoons olive oil
1 onion, chopped
2 garlic cloves, chopped
2 pinches of crushed dried chillies
10 plum tomatoes, skinned, deseeded
  and chopped
1 teaspoon sugar
1 teaspoon vinegar
handful of flat leaf parsley, chopped
salt and pepper
50 g (2 oz) vegetarian Parmesan cheese
  shavings, to serve

Preparation time:
15 minutes

Cooking time:
12 minutes

Serves: **4**

2 tablespoons olive oil
6 large courgettes, thickly sliced
8 spring onions, finely sliced
450 g (14½ oz) dried linguine
vegetarian Parmesan cheese shavings,
  to serve

GREMOLATA:
grated rind of 2 unwaxed lemons
1 tablespoon oil
10 tablespoons chopped flat leaf parsley
2 garlic cloves, crushed

Cook the rigatoni in a large saucepan of lightly salted boiling water for 10–12 minutes, or according to the packet instructions, until al dente.

Meanwhile, heat the oil in a saucepan and fry the onion and garlic until soft but not brown. Stir in the chillies. Add the tomatoes to the onion mixture with the sugar and vinegar and season to taste with salt and pepper. Mix gently and simmer for a few minutes.

Drain the cooked pasta. Stir the parsley into the tomato sauce, then add the sauce to the pasta and mix well. Serve immediately with the Parmesan shavings.

To make the gremolata, mix together all the ingredients in a small bowl.

Heat the oil in a nonstick frying pan and fry the courgette slices over a high heat, stirring, for 10 minutes, or until brown. Add the spring onions and cook for 1–2 minutes.

Meanwhile, cook the pasta in a large saucepan of boiling water for 10–12 minutes, or according to the packet instructions, until al dente. Drain well, then stir in the courgettes, spring onions and gremolata. Serve immediately, topped with Parmesan shavings.

NUTRITIONAL INFORMATION One small tomato provides about one quarter of the daily requirement of vitamin C. The vitamin C content of fruits and vegetables diminishes with storage, preparation and cooking. Cook fresh tomatoes quickly and serve them immediately whenever possible. Some vitamin C does remain in canned tomatoes and tomato purée.

433 kcals (1819 kj) ▪ low GI ▪ source of antioxidants ▪ source of vitamin C

529 kcals (2221 kj) ▪ low GI ▪ source of potassium ▪ source of vitamin C

183 Herbed penne with cherry tomatoes

184 Penne with spring vegetables

Preparation time:
10 minutes

Cooking time:
15 minutes

Serves: **4**

375 g (12 oz) dried penne
200 g (7 oz) cherry tomatoes, halved
2 tablespoons ready-made fresh pesto
1 tablespoon white wine vinegar
2 tablespoons capers, drained
2 tablespoons chopped mixed herbs
   (such as parsley and basil)
salt and pepper
vegetarian Parmesan cheese shavings,
   to serve

Cook the penne in a large saucepan of lightly salted boiling water for 10–12 minutes, or according to the packet instructions, until al dente. Drain thoroughly.

Meanwhile, cook the tomatoes under a preheated hot grill for about 15 minutes until slightly charred and beginning to look dry.

Whiz the pesto, vinegar, capers and herbs in a food processor or blender until almost smooth but still retaining a little texture.

Toss the sauce through the pasta with the tomatoes and season to taste with salt and pepper. Serve immediately with Parmesan shavings.

NUTRITIONAL INFORMATION Lycopene – a very powerful antioxidant found in tomatoes – is a rare nutrient in that cooking increases its potency. Canned tomatoes, tomato purée and tomato juice are all rich in lycopene – but also high in sodium.

375 kcals (1574 kj) ■ **low fat** ■ **low GI** ■ **source of antioxidants** ■ **source of vitamin C**

Preparation time:
30 minutes

Cooking time:
20–25 minutes

Serves: **4**

200 g (7 oz) broccoli florets, divided into
   tiny sprigs
4 young carrots, thinly sliced
200 g (7 oz) frozen petits pois
375 g (12 oz) dried penne
200 g (7 oz) small button mushrooms,
   quartered
6 tablespoons dry white wine
2 tablespoons finely chopped parsley
300 ml (½ pint) low-fat natural yogurt
salt and pepper
1 tablespoon freshly grated vegetarian
   Parmesan cheese, to serve

Cook the broccoli and carrots in a saucepan of lightly salted boiling water for 5–7 minutes until they are tender but still crunchy. Remove with a slotted spoon and drain. Add the petits pois to the water and return to the boil. Simmer for 3–4 minutes, then drain well.

Cook the penne in a large saucepan of lightly salted boiling water for 10–12 minutes, or according to the packet instructions, until al dente.

Meanwhile, put the mushrooms, wine and parsley into a saucepan and season to taste with salt and pepper. Cook for 8–10 minutes, stirring. Add the cooked vegetables and toss over a high heat to heat them through.

Drain the penne thoroughly and transfer to a warmed bowl. Add the yogurt and vegetables and toss together. Divide the pasta between 4 warmed soup bowls and serve immediately with Parmesan shavings.

531 kcals (2228 kj) ■ **low fat** ■ **low GI** ■ **source of antioxidants** ■ **source of potassium**

185 Spaghetti with three herb sauce

186 Vegetarian spaghetti bolognese

Preparation time:
15 minutes

Cooking time:
10–12 minutes

Serves: **4**

3 tablespoons chopped parsley
1 tablespoon chopped tarragon
2 tablespoons chopped basil
1 tablespoon olive oil
1 large garlic clove, crushed
4 tablespoons Vegetable stock
  (see Introduction)
2 tablespoons dry white wine
375 g (12 oz) dried spaghetti
salt and pepper

Put the parsley, tarragon, basil, oil, garlic, stock, wine and salt and pepper to taste into a food processor or blender and whiz until smooth.

Cook the spaghetti in a large saucepan of lightly salted boiling water for 10–12 minutes, or according to the packet instructions, until al dente.

Drain the spaghetti and pile in a warmed bowl. Pour over the herb sauce and toss well, then serve immediately.

Preparation time:
15 minutes

Cooking time:
35–45 minutes

Serves: **2**

1 tablespoon vegetable oil
1 onion, finely chopped
1 garlic clove, finely chopped
1 celery stick, finely chopped
1 carrot, finely chopped
75 g (3 oz) chestnut mushrooms, roughly
  chopped
1 tablespoon tomato purée
400 g (13 oz) can chopped tomatoes
250 ml (8 fl oz) red wine or Vegetable
  Stock (see Introduction)
pinch of dried mixed herbs
1 teaspoon yeast extract
150 g (5 oz) textured vegetable protein
2 tablespoons chopped parsley
200 g (7 oz) dried wholewheat spaghetti
salt and pepper
freshly grated vegetarian Parmesan
  cheese, to serve

Heat the oil in a large, heavy-based saucepan and fry the onion, garlic, celery, carrot and mushrooms for about 5 minutes, or until soft.

Add the tomato purée and fry for 1 minute, then add the tomatoes, wine or stock, mixed herbs, yeast extract and textured vegetable protein. Bring to the boil, then reduce the heat, cover the pan and simmer for 30–40 minutes, or until the textured vegetable protein is tender. Stir in the parsley and season to taste with salt and pepper.

Meanwhile, cook the spaghetti in a large saucepan of lightly salted boiling water for 10–12 minutes, or according to packet instructions, until al dente. Drain well, then spoon on to warmed serving plates. Top with the Bolognese mixture, sprinkle over a little Parmesan and serve immediately.

278 kcals (1167 kj) ■ low fat ■ low GI ■ source of protein

784 kcals (3291 kj) ■ low GI ■ high fibre ■ source of potassium ■ source of protein

187 Spaghetti puttanesca

188 Spinach spaghetti

Preparation time:
10 minutes

Cooking time:
25 minutes

Serves: **2**

1 tablespoon olive oil
1 garlic clove, crushed
pinch of chilli flakes
400 g (13 oz) can chopped tomatoes
50 g (2 oz) pitted black olives, roughly chopped
1 tablespoon tomato purée
1 tablespoon capers
300 g (10 oz) canned flageolet beans, drained and rinsed
175 g (6 oz) dried wholewheat spaghetti
handful of basil leaves
salt and pepper
vegetarian Parmesan cheese shavings, to serve (optional)

Heat the oil in a nonstick frying pan and fry the garlic and chilli flakes for 1–2 minutes. Add the tomatoes, olives, tomato purée, capers and beans. Reduce the heat and simmer for 20 minutes, or until the sauce is thick. Season to taste with salt and pepper.

Meanwhile, cook the spaghetti in a large saucepan of lightly salted boiling water for 10–12 minutes, or according to the packet instructions, until al dente.

Drain the spaghetti and return it to the pan. Stir in the sauce and the basil leaves and toss well. Sprinkle with Parmesan shavings, if liked, and serve immediately.

NUTRITIONAL INFORMATION **Puttanesca, or 'tart's sauce' takes only minutes to prepare. Use fresh plum tomatoes when in season for increased vitamin C content.**

592 kcals (2484 kj) ■ **low GI** ■ **high fibre**

Preparation time:
10 minutes

Cooking time:
10–12 minutes

Serves: **3**

250 g (8 oz) dried spaghetti
1 onion, chopped
250 g (8 oz) spinach, chopped
150 g (5 oz) low-fat natural yogurt
125 g (4 oz) vegetarian quark cheese
1 teaspoon lemon juice
¼ teaspoon grated nutmeg
salt and pepper

Cook the spaghetti in a large saucepan of lightly salted water boiling water for 10–12 minutes, or according to the packet instructions, until al dente.

Meanwhile, heat a frying pan and dry-fry the onion, stirring constantly, until soft but not browned. Add the spinach and cook for 2–3 minutes. Stir in the yogurt, quark, lemon juice, nutmeg and salt and pepper to taste and cook over a low heat without boiling. Drain the spaghetti thoroughly and add it to the hot spinach sauce. Toss well, then serve immediately.

376 kcals (1578 kj) ■ **low fat** ■ **low GI** ■ **source of iron**

189 Rocket risotto

190 Green herb risotto

Preparation time:
5 minutes

Cooking time:
25–30 minutes

Serves: **4**

1 teaspoon olive oil
1 onion, finely chopped
300 g (10 oz) arborio rice
1.2 litres (2 pints) Vegetable Stock (see
Introduction), simmering
50 g (2 oz) rocket leaves, plus extra to
garnish
salt and pepper

Heat the oil in a large nonstick frying pan and fry the onion for 2–3 minutes until it is beginning to soften. Add the rice and cook, stirring, for 1 minute.

Add the stock, a ladleful at a time, stirring constantly, allowing each ladleful to be absorbed before adding the next. Continue until all the stock has been absorbed and the rice is creamy but still firm to the bite. This will take about 20 minutes.

Stir in the rocket, reserving 4 leaves for garnish, and cook just until the leaves start to wilt. Season to taste with salt and pepper. To serve, garnish each portion with a rocket leaf.

Preparation time:
5 minutes

Cooking time:
25 minutes

Serves: **4**

1 tablespoon olive oil
1 onion, finely chopped
1 garlic clove, chopped
300 g (10 oz) arborio rice
1 litre (1¾ pints) Vegetable Stock (see
Introduction), simmering
handful of parsley, chopped
handful of basil, chopped
handful of oregano, chopped
handful of thyme, chopped
25 g (1 oz) vegetarian Parmesan cheese,
freshly grated
salt and pepper
sage sprigs, to garnish

Heat the butter and oil in a large saucepan and fry the onion and garlic for 2–3 minutes until they begin to soften. Add the rice and cook, stirring, for 1 minute.

Add the stock, a ladleful at a time, stirring constantly, allowing each ladleful to be absorbed before adding the next. Continue until all the stock has been absorbed and the rice is creamy but still firm to the bite. This will take about 20 minutes.

Add the herbs and Parmesan. Season to taste with salt and pepper and stir well. Serve immediately, garnished with sage sprigs.

NUTRITIONAL INFORMATION The main 'active' ingredients in herbs are their volatile oils and various phytochemicals, which offer a huge range of therapeutic benefits. Fresh parsley freezes easily and can simply be crumbled into recipes when frozen.

290 kcals (1222 kj) ■ **low fat** ■ **source of antioxidants** ■ **source of iron**

335 kcals (1417 kj) ■ **low fat** ■ **source of calcium**

191 Cashew and green pepper risotto

192 Red rice and pumpkin risotto

Preparation time:
10 minutes

Cooking time:
45 minutes–1 hour

Serves: **4**

2 teaspoons vegetable oil
1 onion, finely sliced
1 green pepper, cored, deseeded and finely sliced
125 g (4 oz) sweetcorn kernels
300 g (10 oz) brown rice
900 ml (1½ pints) Vegetable Stock (see Introduction), simmering
1 tablespoon soy sauce
125 g (4 oz) unsalted cashew nuts

Heat the oil in a large frying pan and gently fry the onion and pepper for about 5 minutes until softened. Add the sweetcorn and rice and cook, stirring, for 2–3 minutes.

Stir in the stock and bring to the boil, then reduce the heat and simmer, uncovered, for 30–40 minutes until the rice is tender.

Stir in the soy sauce and cashew nuts and cook for a further 5–10 minutes until all the stock has been absorbed. Serve immediately.

NUTRITIONAL INFORMATION Research suggests that eating a small handful of unsalted nuts several days a week can help to lower cholesterol levels and reduce the risk of a heart attack. Although high in fat, nuts make a healthy substitute for crisps and biscuits.

421 kcals (1768 kj) ▪ **low GI** ▪ **high fibre** ▪ **source of protein**

Preparation time:
20 minutes

Cooking time:
35 minutes

Serves: **4**

1 litre (1¾ pints) Vegetable Stock (see Introduction)
250 g (8 oz) Camargue red rice
1 tablespoon olive oil
1 onion, finely chopped
2 garlic cloves, finely chopped
750 g (1½ lb) pumpkin, peeled, deseeded and diced
5 tablespoons finely chopped basil or oregano, plus extra leaves to garnish
50 g (2 oz) vegetarian Parmesan cheese, freshly grated
salt and pepper
vegetarian Parmesan cheese shavings, to serve

Bring the stock to the boil in a saucepan, then add the rice and simmer for 35 minutes.

Meanwhile, heat the oil in a frying pan and fry the onion for about 5 minutes until softened. Stir in the garlic, pumpkin and a little salt and pepper, then cover the pan and cook over a medium heat for 10 minutes, stirring occasionally, until the pumpkin is softened.

Drain the rice and reserve the cooking liquid. Stir the chopped herbs into the frying pan along with the vegetables, add the drained rice and grated Parmesan. Taste and adjust the seasoning. Moisten with the reserved rice liquid if needed. Spoon the risotto into warmed shallow dishes and garnish with herb leaves and Parmesan shavings.

345 kcals (1435 kj) ▪ **low fat** ▪ **high fibre** ▪ **source of antioxidants**

193 Mushroom risotto

194 Wholemeal crêpes with wild mushrooms

Preparation time:
30 minutes

Cooking time:
about 30 minutes

Serves: **4**

15 g (½ oz) low-fat spread
1 onion, sliced
250 g (8 oz) brown medium-grain rice
150 ml (¼ pint) dry white wine
600 ml (1 pint) Vegetable Stock (see Introduction), simmering
250 g (8 oz) mushrooms, sliced
1 tablespoon chopped basil
1 tablespoon freshly grated vegetarian Parmesan cheese
salt and pepper

Heat the low-fat spread in a saucepan and fry the onion until golden. Stir in the rice and cook for 5 minutes, stirring frequently.

Add the wine, bring to the boil and continue boiling until it is well reduced. Stir in a ladleful of the stock, the mushrooms, basil and salt and pepper to taste. Continue adding the stock and stirring until it has all been absorbed and the rice is cooked. Stir in the grated Parmesan, and serve immediately.

Preparation time:
20 minutes

Cooking time:
30 minutes

Oven temperature:
180°C (350°F) Gas Mark 4

Serves: **4**

50 g (2 oz) plain wholemeal flour
150 ml (¼ pint) semi-skimmed milk
1 small egg, beaten
1 teaspoon olive oil
salt and pepper
flat leaf parsley sprigs, to garnish

FILLING:
1 bunch of spring onions, finely chopped
1 garlic clove, chopped
125 g (4 oz) wild mushrooms, torn
50 g (2 oz) low-fat curd cheese
1 tablespoon chopped flat leaf parsley

To make the crêpe batter, put the flour, milk and egg into a food processor or blender with salt and pepper to taste and whiz until smooth, or whisk by hand.

Pour a few drops of oil into a frying pan. Heat the pan, pour in a ladleful of batter and cook for 1 minute. Carefully flip the crêpe and cook the second side. Slide the crêpe out of the pan on to a piece of greaseproof paper. Make 3 more crêpes in the same way, adding a few more drops of oil to the pan between each one. Stack the crêpes between greaseproof paper.

Meanwhile, to make the filling, put all the ingredients into a small saucepan and cook, stirring occasionally, for 5 minutes.

Divide the filling between the crêpes, reserving a little of the mixture for serving, and roll them up. Transfer to an ovenproof dish and cook in a preheated oven, 180°C (350°F), Gas Mark 4, for 20 minutes. Serve with the remaining mixture and garnish with parsley sprigs.

NUTRITIONAL INFORMATION The high fibre content of this risotto is largely due to the addition of brown rice and mushrooms.

504 kcals (2107 kj) ■ **low fat** ■ **low GI** ■ **high fibre** ■ **source of potassium**

99 kcals (416 kj) ■ **low fat** ■ **low carb** ■ **low GI** ■ **source of iron** ■ **source of potassium**

195 Tortillas with red onion salsa

Preparation time: **10 minutes**	**2 small flour tortillas** **vegetable oil, for brushing** **green salad, to serve**
Cooking time: **5 minutes**	RED ONION SALSA: **25 g (1 oz) ricotta cheese**
Serves: **1**	**½ red onion, finely sliced** **1 tomato, finely chopped** **¼ green chilli, finely chopped** **1 tablespoon chopped coriander leaves**

First, to make the salsa, mix together all the ingredients in a bowl.

Heat a griddle pan. Brush the tortillas with a little oil. Put on the griddle and cook very briefly on each side.

Spread half the salsa over one half of each tortilla, then fold over the second half. Serve with a green salad.

196 Tortillas with minted chilli and aubergine

Preparation time: **10 minutes**	**4 tablespoons olive oil** **1 aubergine, thinly sliced** **small handful of mint, chopped**
Cooking time: **10 minutes**	**small handful of parsley, chopped** **2 tablespoons snipped chives** **1 green chilli, deseeded and thinly sliced**
Serves: **2**	**200 g (7 oz) Greek yogurt** **2 tablespoons low-fat mayonnaise** **2 large flour tortillas** **7 cm (3 inch) length of cucumber, thinly sliced** **salt and pepper** **paprika, to garnish**

Heat the oil in a frying pan and fry the aubergine for about 10 minutes until golden. Drain and set aside to cool.

Mix the herbs with the chilli, yogurt and mayonnaise in a bowl and season to taste with salt and pepper.

Arrange the fried aubergine slices over the tortillas and spread with the yogurt mixture. Arrange the cucumber slices on top. Roll up each tortilla, sprinkle with paprika and serve.

318 kcals (1344 kj) ▪ **low fat** ▪ **source of antioxidants** ▪ **source of iron**

498 kcals (2082 kj) ▪ **low carb** ▪ **low GI** ▪ **source of antioxidants**

197 Couscous with grilled vegetables

198 Fragrant vegetable tagine

Preparation time:	
15 minutes, plus standing	**300 g (10 oz) couscous**
	500 ml (17 fl oz) boiling water
	2 red peppers, cored, deseeded and
Cooking time:	**quartered**
10 minutes	**1 orange pepper, cored, deseeded and**
	quartered
Serves: **4**	**6 baby courgettes, halved lengthways**
	2 red onions, cut into wedges
	24 cherry tomatoes
	2 garlic cloves, finely sliced
	2 tablespoons olive oil
	100 g (3½ oz) asparagus, trimmed
	grated rind and juice of 1 lemon
	4 tablespoons chopped herbs (such as
	parsley or mint)
	salt and pepper
	lemon wedge, to serve

Preparation time:	
15 minutes	**½ tablespoon olive oil**
	½ red onion, thinly sliced
	1 garlic clove, crushed
Cooking time:	**pinch of ground cumin**
30–35 minutes	**1 teaspoon harissa**
	50 g (2 oz) ready-to-eat dried apricots,
Serves: **2**	**roughly chopped**
	1 large carrot, thickly sliced
	½ red pepper, cored, deseeded and
	roughly chopped
	200 ml (7 fl oz) Vegetable Stock (see
	Introduction)
	300 g (10 oz) canned chickpeas, drained
	and rinsed
	125 g (4 oz) cherry tomatoes, halved
	1 tablespoon chopped coriander leaves
	1 tablespoon chopped mint leaves
	salt and pepper
	couscous, to serve

Tip the couscous into a large heatproof bowl, pour over the measurement water, cover and set aside for 10 minutes.

Meanwhile, put the peppers, courgettes, onions, tomatoes and garlic into a grill pan in a single layer, drizzle over the oil and cook under a preheated hot grill for 5–6 minutes, turning occasionally.

Add the asparagus to the pan and continue to grill for 2–3 minutes until the vegetables are tender and lightly charred. When they are cool enough to handle, remove the skins from the peppers and discard.

Fork through the couscous to separate the grains. Toss with the vegetables, lemon rind and juice and herbs, season to taste with salt and pepper and serve immediately.

Heat the oil in a large saucepan and fry the onion for about 5 minutes, or until soft. Add the garlic, cumin and harissa and cook for 1 minute.

Stir in the apricots, carrot and pepper, then pour over the stock and bring to the boil. Season to taste with salt and pepper. Reduce the heat, cover the pan and simmer for 15 minutes.

Add the chickpeas and tomatoes and cook for a further 10 minutes, or until the vegetables are just tender. Stir in the coriander and mint and serve with couscous.

241 kcals (1007 kj) ■ **low fat** ■ **low GI** ■ **source of antioxidants** ■ **source of vitamin C**

280 kcals (1188 kj) ■ **low fat** ■ **high fibre** ■ **source of antioxidants** ■ **source of iron** ■ **source of vitamin C**

199 Mini falafel salad

Preparation time:
15 minutes

Cooking time:
5 minutes

Serves: **4**

2 x 400 g (13 oz) cans chickpeas, drained
  and rinsed
2 teaspoons ground coriander
2 teaspoons ground cumin
2 garlic cloves, crushed
2 tablespoons chopped coriander leaves
1 egg yolk, beaten
2 tablespoons olive oil
lemon wedges, to garnish
mini pitta breads, to serve (optional)

SALAD:
3 Little Gem lettuces, torn into bite-sized
  pieces
½ cucumber, sliced

DRESSING:
300 g (10 oz) low-fat natural yogurt
3 tablespoons chopped mint
3 tablespoons chopped parsley
salt and pepper

Place two-thirds of the chickpeas into a food processor or blender with the ground coriander, cumin and garlic and whiz until almost smooth. Stir in the coriander leaves and the egg yolk.

Using your hands, form the mixture into 16 small balls and brush with the oil. Cook under a preheated hot grill for 3–4 minutes until golden.

Divide the lettuce, cucumber, the remaining chickpeas and the falafel between 4 plates.

Mix together all the dressing ingredients. Serve the falafel salad with the dressing, the pitta breads, if liked, and garnish with lemon wedges.

267 kcals (1123 kj) ▪ low GI ▪ high fibre ▪ source of
iron ▪ source of protein

200 Nut koftas with minted yogurt

Preparation time:
15 minutes

Cooking time:
10 minutes

Serves: **4**

5–6 tablespoons groundnut oil
1 onion, chopped
½ teaspoon crushed chilli flakes
2 garlic cloves, roughly chopped
1 tablespoon medium curry paste
425 g (14 oz) can borlotti or cannellini
  beans, drained and rinsed
125 g (4 oz) ground almonds
75 g (3 oz) chopped honey-roast almonds
1 small egg
200 g (7 oz) Greek yogurt
2 tablespoons chopped mint
1 tablespoon lemon juice
salt and pepper
mint sprigs, to garnish
warm naan bread, to serve

Soak 8 bamboo skewers in hot water. Heat 3 tablespoons of the oil in a saucepan and fry the onion for 4 minutes. Add the chilli flakes, garlic and curry paste and fry for 1 minute. Whiz the mixture in a food processor or blender with the beans, ground and chopped almonds, egg and salt and pepper to taste until it starts to bind together.

With lightly floured hands, take about one-eighth of the mixture and mould it around a skewer, to make a sausage about 2.5 cm (1 inch) thick. Make 7 more koftas. Put the koftas on a foil-lined grill rack and brush with 1 tablespoon of the remaining oil. Cook under a preheated moderate grill for about 5 minutes until golden, turning once.

Meanwhile, mix together the yogurt and mint in a small bowl. In a separate bowl, mix together the remaining oil, lemon juice and salt and pepper to taste. Brush the koftas with the lemon dressing and serve with the yogurt dressing on warm naan bread, garnished with mint sprigs.

704 kcals (2943 kj) ▪ low fat ▪ low GI ▪ high fibre ▪
source of iron ▪ source of protein

201 Mushroom and pea bhaji

Preparation time:
15 minutes

Cooking time:
20 minutes

Serves: **4**

2 tablespoons vegetable oil
50 g (2 oz) onion, finely sliced
¼ teaspoon cumin seeds, crushed
¼ teaspoon mustard seeds
125 g (4 oz) tomatoes, chopped
1 green chilli, deseeded and finely
  chopped
425 g (14 oz) button mushrooms, halved,
  or quartered if large
150 g (5 oz) frozen peas
½ teaspoon chilli powder
¼ teaspoon turmeric
1 red pepper, cored, deseeded and
  chopped
4 garlic cloves, crushed
2 tablespoons chopped coriander leaves
chopped spring onions or chives,
  to garnish

Heat the oil in a saucepan and gently fry the onion for 2–3 minutes until it begins to soften. Add the cumin and mustard seeds and fry, stirring, for 2 minutes.

Add the tomatoes, chilli, mushrooms and peas. Stir and cook for 2 minutes. Stir in the chilli powder and turmeric, mix well, then cook, uncovered, for 5–7 minutes.

Add the pepper, garlic and coriander leaves and cook for a further 5 minutes until the mixture is dry. Serve, garnished with spring onions or chives.

113 kcals (470 kj) ▪ low fat ▪ low carb ▪ low GI ▪
high fibre ▪ source of iron

202 Stuffed tomatoes

Preparation time:
15 minutes, plus standing

Cooking time:
about 1¼ hours

Oven temperature:
**220°C (425°F) Gas Mark 7/
200°C (400°F) Gas Mark 6**

Serves: **4**

1 green pepper, cored, deseeded and
  quartered
125 g (4 oz) couscous
4 beef tomatoes
4 spring onions, diagonally sliced
1 tablespoon white wine vinegar
2 tablespoons wholegrain mustard
salt and pepper
dill sprigs, to garnish
mixed herb salad, to serve

Slightly flatten the pepper quarters and put on a baking sheet. Roast in a preheated oven, 220°C (425°F), Gas Mark 7, for 30–40 minutes until the pepper is slightly charred. When the pepper quarters are cool enough to handle, remove the skin and discard.

Put the couscous into a heatproof bowl. Pour over enough boiling water to cover, stir, cover and set aside for 10 minutes. Meanwhile, cut the top off each tomato and reserve. Carefully core and deseed the tomatoes, reserving the flesh. Heat a nonstick frying pan and dry-fry the spring onions for 3 minutes. Set aside.

Chop the pepper quarters and stir into the couscous with the spring onions, vinegar, mustard and tomato flesh. Season to taste with salt and pepper, then divide the mixture between the tomatoes. Top each tomato with its lid.

Put the tomatoes into a small roasting tin and cook in a preheated oven, 200°C (400°F), Gas Mark 6, for 30 minutes. Garnish with dill sprigs and serve with a mixed herb salad.

116 kcals (488 kj) ▪ low fat ▪ source of antioxidants ▪
source of vitamin C

203 Leek filo tarts

204 Herby bean cakes

Preparation time:
10 minutes, plus standing

Cooking time:
30 minutes

Oven temperature:
200°C (400°F) Gas Mark 6

Serves: 4

8 sun-dried tomatoes
2 leeks, sliced into rings
300 ml (½ pint) white wine
2 tablespoons semi-skimmed milk
1 small egg, separated
50 g (2 oz) low-fat vegetarian soft cheese
12 x 15 cm (6 inch) squares of filo pastry,
    defrosted if frozen
salt and pepper

TO SERVE:
vine tomatoes (optional)
sliced red onion (optional)

Put the tomatoes into a small heatproof bowl and pour over enough boiling water to cover. Set aside for 20 minutes.

Meanwhile, put the leeks into a saucepan with the wine, bring to the boil and simmer until all the wine has evaporated. Remove the leeks from the heat and stir in the milk, egg yolk and soft cheese. Season well with salt and pepper.

Brush a pastry square with a little egg white and use it to line the base and sides of a 10 cm (4 inch) tart tin. Brush 2 more squares and lay these on top, each at a slightly different angle from the first, allowing the edges to flop over the rim. Line 3 more tart tins in the same way, using up all the pastry squares.

Half-fill each pastry case with a spoonful of the cooked leek mixture. Put 2 rehydrated tomatoes on top, then cover them with the remaining leeks. Season well with salt and pepper and cook in a preheated oven, 200°C (400°F), Gas Mark 6, for 20 minutes, covering the tarts with foil after 10 minutes. Serve the tarts with vine tomatoes and sliced red onion, if liked.

Preparation time:
10 minutes

Cooking time:
10–15 minutes

Oven temperature:
200°C (400°F) Gas Mark 6

Serves: 4

2 x 400 g (13 oz) cans cannellini beans,
    drained and rinsed
2 eggs, beaten
1 bunch of spring onions, finely chopped
4 tablespoons chopped herbs (such as
    sage, parsley or thyme)
50 g (2 oz) Stilton cheese, crumbled
4 tablespoons plain flour
50 g (2 oz) fine white breadcrumbs
2 tablespoons olive oil, plus extra for
    oiling
salt and pepper
4 parsley sprigs, to garnish
tomato, cucumber and onion salad,
    to serve

Put the beans into a food processor or blender and whiz until almost smooth. Add half the beaten egg and whiz again. Stir in the spring onions, herbs and Stilton. Season to taste with salt and pepper.

Using your hands, shape the mixture into 8 balls, then flatten them slightly. Coat the patties in flour. Dip them in the remaining egg, then into the breadcrumbs, to coat them evenly. Put on a lightly oiled baking sheet and drizzle with the oil.

Cook the bean cakes in a preheated oven 200°C (400°F), Gas Mark 6, for 10–15 minutes until golden and piping hot. Garnish each serving with a parsley sprig and serve with a tomato and cucumber salad.

135 kcals (565 kj) ■ low fat ■ source of antioxidants ■ source of calcium

352 kcals (1474 kj) ■ low GI ■ high fibre ■ source of calcium

205 Celeriac remoulade with asparagus

Preparation time:
10 minutes

Cooking time:
about 10 minutes

Serves: **4**

500 g (1 lb) celeriac
375 g (12 oz) potatoes
1 teaspoon olive oil
500 g (1 lb) asparagus, trimmed

REMOULADE SAUCE:
1 tablespoon low-fat mayonnaise
150 ml (¼ pint) low-fat natural yogurt
1 teaspoon Dijon mustard
6 cocktail gherkins, finely chopped
2 tablespoons chopped capers
2 tablespoons chopped tarragon
salt and pepper

Peel the celeriac and potatoes and cut into matchsticks, but keep the 2 vegetables separate. Cook the celeriac in a saucepan of lightly salted boiling water for 2 minutes, or until softened. Add the potatoes and cook for a further 2 minutes, or until just tender. Drain the vegetables and refresh under cold running water.

Meanwhile, mix together the ingredients for the sauce in a bowl and set aside.

Heat the oil in a frying pan and fry the asparagus for 2–3 minutes until it just begins to colour.

Mix the celeriac and potato with the sauce and spoon on to 4 plates. Top with the asparagus spears and serve immediately.

NUTRITIONAL INFORMATION Celeriac is a useful source of folate – a powerful antioxidant that is good for our hearts – and vitamin C. It is also a valuable source of fibre and using washed, unpeeled new baby potatoes in this recipe will boost that fibre and vitamin C content.

262 kcals (1095 kj) ■ **low fat** ■ **low carb** ■ **high fibre** ■
source of antioxidants ■ **source of vitamin C**

206 Spinach, butter bean and ricotta frittata

Preparation time:
10 minutes

Cooking time:
10–15 minutes

Serves: **2**

1 teaspoon olive oil
1 onion, sliced
400 g (13 oz) can butter beans, drained and rinsed
200 g (7 oz) baby spinach
4 eggs, beaten
50 g (2 oz) ricotta cheese
salt (optional) and pepper
tomato and red onion salad, to serve

Heat the oil in a medium frying pan and gently fry the onion for 3–4 minutes until softened. Add the butter beans and spinach and heat gently for 2–3 minutes until the spinach has wilted.

Pour the eggs over the vegetables, add the ricotta and season to taste with salt, if using, and pepper. Cook until the eggs are almost set, then put the pan under a preheated hot grill and cook for 1–2 minutes until the top of the frittata is golden and set. Cut into wedges and serve with a tomato and onion salad.

359 kcals (1503 kj) ■ **low GI** ■ **source of calcium** ■
source of iron

207 Tomato ratatouille gratin

208 Smoked tofu and apricot sausages

Preparation time:
15 minutes

Cooking time:
about 1 hour

Oven temperature:
220°C (425°F) Gas Mark 7

Serves: **6**

4 tablespoons olive oil
2 onions, finely chopped
2 garlic cloves, crushed (optional)
1 aubergine, diced
500 g (1 lb) courgettes, diced
3 red peppers, cored, deseeded and roughly chopped
1 yellow pepper, cored, deseeded and roughly chopped
2 green peppers, cored, deseeded and roughly chopped
2 x 400 g (13 oz) cans chopped tomatoes
2 teaspoons dried mixed herbs
50 g (2 oz) dried breadcrumbs
25 g (1 oz) vegetarian Cheddar cheese, grated
1 tablespoon freshly grated vegetarian Parmesan cheese
salt and pepper

Heat the oil in a large saucepan and gently fry the onions until soft and golden brown. Add the garlic, if using, and cook for a further 1 minute.

Add the aubergine and courgettes to the pan and fry until soft and beginning to brown. Add the peppers to the pan and stir to coat in the oil. Cook for 5 minutes until the peppers have softened. Add the tomatoes and bring to a fast boil. Reduce the heat and add salt and pepper to taste and the herbs. Half-cover the pan and simmer for 10 minutes.

Spoon the ratatouille mixture into a large ovenproof dish and level the top. Mix the breadcrumbs with the Cheddar and Parmesan and sprinkle on top. Bake in a preheated oven, 220°C (425°F), Gas Mark 7, for 20–25 minutes, or until the breadcrumb mixture is golden brown and bubbling.

226 kcals (945 kj) ▪ **low carb** ▪ **low GI** ▪ **high fibre** ▪ **source of antioxidants** ▪ **source of vitamin C**

Preparation time:
20 minutes

Cooking time:
10 minutes

Serves: **4**

225 g (7½ oz) smoked firm tofu, drained
3 teaspoons olive oil, plus a little extra for frying
1 large onion, roughly chopped
2 celery sticks, roughly chopped
100 g (3½ oz) ready-to-eat dried apricots, roughly chopped
50 g (2 oz) breadcrumbs
1 egg
1 tablespoon chopped sage
salt and pepper

TO SERVE:
potato wedges (optional)
tomato relish (optional)

Pat the tofu dry on kitchen paper and tear it into chunks. Heat the oil in a frying pan and fry the onion and celery for 5 minutes until softened. Put the onion and celery into a food processor, add the tofu and apricots and whiz to a chunky paste.

Tip the mixture into a bowl and add the breadcrumbs, egg and sage. Season to taste with salt and pepper and beat well until evenly combined. Divide the mixture into 8 portions. Using lightly floured hands, shape each portion into a sausage, pressing the mixture together firmly.

Heat a little oil in a nonstick frying pan and fry the sausages for about 5 minutes, or until golden. Serve immediately with potato wedges and tomato relish, if liked.

217 kcals (909 kj) ▪ **low fat** ▪ **high fibre** ▪ **source of calcium** ▪ **source of phytoestrogens**

9 Desserts

209 Mini strawberry shortcakes

Preparation time:
20 minutes, plus chilling

Serves: **4**

250 g (8 oz) strawberries
8 low-fat digestive biscuits
4 teaspoons low-sugar strawberry jam
250 g (8 oz) low-fat cream cheese
**2 teaspoons icing sugar, plus extra
    to decorate**

Reserve 4 strawberries for decoration. Hull and slice the remaining strawberries. Fan the 4 reserved strawberries.

Spread a digestive biscuit with 1 teaspoon of the strawberry jam. Beat the cream cheese in a bowl to soften it and stir in the icing sugar. Spread one-eighth of the mixture over the biscuit. Put a few strawberry slices on top of the cream cheese, then cover with more of the cream cheese mixture and a second biscuit. Lay a fanned strawberry on top and dust with icing sugar. Repeat to make 3 more shortcakes. Chill for at least 1 hour before serving.

255 kcals (1071 kj) ■ **low fat** ■ **source of antioxidants**

210 Peach and raspberry tartlets

Preparation time:
15 minutes

Cooking time:
8–10 minutes

Oven temperature:
190°C (375°F) Gas Mark 5

Serves: **4**

15 g (½ oz) butter, melted
**4 sheets of filo pastry, defrosted if frozen,
    each about 25 cm (10 inches) square**
125 ml (4 fl oz) double cream
1 tablespoon soft brown sugar
**2 peaches, skinned, halved, stoned and
    diced**
50 g (2 oz) raspberries
icing sugar, to decorate

Grease 4 sections of a deep muffin tin with the melted butter. Cut a sheet of filo pastry in half, then across into 4 equal-sized squares. Use these filo squares to line 1 muffin tin section, arranging them at slightly different angles. Press them down well, tucking the pastry into the tin neatly. Repeat with the remaining pastry.

Bake the filo pastry tartlets in a preheated oven, 190°C (375°F), Gas Mark 5, for 8–10 minutes, or until golden. Carefully remove the tartlet cases from the tins and cool on a wire rack.

Pour the cream into a bowl and add the brown sugar, then whip it lightly until it holds its shape. Spoon the cream into the tartlet cases and top with the peaches and raspberries. Dust with icing sugar and serve immediately.

COOK'S NOTES To skin peaches, put them into a heatproof bowl and pour over freshly boiling water to cover. Leave for 30–60 seconds, depending on the ripeness of the fruit (the peel on ripe fruit loosens more quickly). Drain the peaches and slit their skins with the point of a knife, then they will slip off easily.

207 kcals (867 kj) ■ **low carb** ■ **source of antioxidants**

211 Summer pudding

Preparation time:
30 minutes, plus soaking
and chilling

Cooking time:
10–15 minutes

Serves: **8**

500 g (1 lb) mixed blackberries
and blackcurrants
3 tablespoons clear honey
125 g (4 oz) raspberries
125 g (4 oz) strawberries
8 slices of wholemeal bread, crusts
removed
low-fat yogurt, to serve

TO DECORATE:
redcurrants
mint sprigs

Put the blackberries, blackcurrants and honey into a heavy-based saucepan and cook gently for 10–15 minutes until tender, stirring occasionally. Add the raspberries and strawberries and allow to cool. Strain the fruit through a nylon sieve, reserving the juice.

Cut 3 circles of bread to fit the base, middle and top of a 900 ml (1½ pint) pudding basin. Shape the remaining bread to fit around the sides of the basin. Soak all the bread in the reserved fruit juice.

Line the bottom of the basin with the smallest circle of bread, then arrange the shaped bread around the sides. Pour in half the fruit and put the middle-sized circle of bread on top. Cover with the remaining fruit, then top with the largest bread circle. Fold over any bread protruding from the basin. Cover the pudding with a saucer small enough to fit inside the basin and put a 500 g (1 lb) weight on top. Leave in the refrigerator overnight.

To serve, turn the pudding on to a serving plate and pour over any remaining fruit juice. Serve with low-fat yogurt and decorate with redcurrants and mint sprigs.

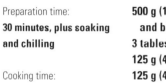
124 kcals (520 kj) ■ **low fat** ■ **low GI** ■ **high fibre** ■
source of antioxidants

212 Mini nectarine and blueberry tarts

Preparation time:
15 minutes

Cooking time:
6–8 minutes

Oven temperature:
180°C (350°F) Gas Mark 4

Serves: **12**

25 g (1 oz) butter
2 teaspoons olive oil
4 sheets of filo pastry, defrosted if frozen,
each about 30 x 18 cm (12 x 7 inches), or
65 g (2½ oz) total weight
2 tablespoons low-sugar red berry jam
juice of ½ orange
4 ripe nectarines, halved, stoned
and sliced
150 g (5 oz) blueberries
sifted icing sugar, for dusting
fromage frais or yogurt ice cream,
to serve (optional)

Melt the butter with the oil in a small saucepan.

Unroll the pastry and separate into sheets. Brush lightly with the butter mixture, then cut into 24 pieces, each 10 x 8 cm (4 x 3½ inches). Arrange a piece in each of the sections of a deep 12-section muffin tin, then add a second piece at a slightly different angle.

Bake the tart cases in a preheated oven, 180°C (350°F), Gas Mark 4, for 6–8 minutes until golden.

Meanwhile, warm the jam and orange juice in a saucepan, then add the nectarines and blueberries and warm through.

Carefully lift the tart cases out of the muffin tin and transfer them to a serving dish. Fill with the warm fruit and dust with sifted icing sugar. Serve with fromage frais or yogurt ice cream, if liked.

69 kcals (289 kj) ■ **low fat** ■ **low carb** ■ **low GI** ■
source of antioxidants

213 Fig and honey pots

214 Burgundy peaches

Preparation time:
10 minutes, plus chilling

Serves: **4**

6 fresh figs, thinly sliced
450 ml (¾ pint) low-fat natural yogurt

TO SERVE:
4 tablespoons clear honey
25 g (1 oz) chopped pistachio nuts

Arrange the fig slices snugly at the bottom of 4 glasses or glass bowls. Spoon the yogurt over the figs and chill for about 10–15 minutes.

To serve, drizzle 1 tablespoon of the honey over each dessert and sprinkle chopped pistachio nuts on top.

NUTRITIONAL INFORMATION Honey has been used as a natural sweetener for many centuries. It has a higher fructose content than cane or beet sugar, but in nutritional terms it is little different from any other sugar.

213 kcals (896 kj) ■ **low fat** ■ **high fibre** ■ **source of antioxidants**

Preparation time:
20 minutes

Cooking time:
25 minutes

Serves: **4**

1 orange
3 tablespoons clear honey
125 ml (4 fl oz) water
½ cinnamon stick
1 clove
grated rind of ½ lemon
300 ml (½ pint) red Burgundy wine
4 large peaches, skinned, halved and stoned, or canned peaches in natural juice
1 tablespoon arrowroot or cornflour
mint sprigs, to decorate

Pare the rind from the orange and reserve. Cut the orange in half and squeeze out the juice.

Put the honey, measurement water, cinnamon stick, clove and orange juice into a large saucepan. Add the lemon rind and a thin strip of orange rind. Cover the pan and bring to the boil over a high heat. Add the wine and peaches, return to the boil, then reduce the heat and simmer for 20 minutes.

When the peaches are tender, lift them out of the cooking liquid with a slotted spoon and allow to cool slightly. Slice each peach half and fan out the segments.

Blend the arrowroot with a little water until smooth. Stir it into the cooking liquid and bring to the boil, stirring constantly until thickened. Strain the sauce into a jug. Pour a little of the sauce on to 4 individual dessert plates. Divide the peaches between each plate and decorate with pieces of the cinnamon stick and mint sprigs. Serve hot or chilled.

129 kcals (540 kj) ■ **low fat** ■ **low GI** ■ **source of vitamin C**

215 Poached pears

216 Griddled apples with frozen yogurt

Preparation time:
10–15 minutes, plus chilling

Cooking time:
about 1¾ hours

Oven temperature:
160°C (325°F) Gas Mark 3

Serves: **4**

4 pears, peeled but stalks left intact
250 ml (8 fl oz) red wine
100 g (3½ oz) caster sugar
1 long sliver of lemon rind, plus extra to decorate
125–250 ml (4–8 fl oz) water
lemon balm sprigs, to decorate

Put the pears into a deep ovenproof casserole just large enough to hold them standing up.

Put the wine, sugar and lemon rind into a small saucepan, bring to the boil and cook, stirring, until the sugar has dissolved. Pour the syrup over the pears and add enough of the measurement water to come just level with the stalks. Cover the dish and bake in a preheated oven, 160°C (325°F), Gas Mark 3, for 1½ hours, or until the pears are tender when tested with a fine skewer.

Remove the pears from the oven and allow to cool. Cover the casserole and chill, spooning the syrup over the pears from time to time. Serve the pears decorated with lemon balm sprigs and lemon rind.

Preparation time:
5 minutes

Cooking time:
6–8 minutes

Serves: **4**

4 Braeburn apples
spun sugar, to decorate (optional)
ready-made low-fat frozen yogurt, to serve

Heat a griddle pan. Cut the apples into quarters and remove the cores. Cut each quarter in half again to create 8 wedges from each apple. Put on the griddle and cook for 3–4 minutes on each side.

Remove the apples from the griddle and put into a serving bowl or on individual plates. Serve with a generous scoop of low-fat frozen yogurt and decorate with spun sugar, if liked.

COOK'S NOTES Pears are rich in both soluble and insoluble fibre. Soluble fibre helps lower cholesterol, while insoluble fibre keeps the digestive system moving and healthy.

171 kcals (719 kj) ■ **low fat** ■ **low GI** ■ **high fibre** ■ **source of vitamin C**

130 kcals (554 kj) ■ **low fat** ■ **high fibre** ■ **source of calcium**

217 Griddled mango with fresh lime juice

Preparation time:
10 minutes

Cooking time:
10 minutes

Serves: **4**

4 mangoes
2 limes, cut into wedges
lime rind, to decorate
Greek yogurt, to serve (optional)

Heat a griddle pan. Using a sharp knife, remove the skin from the mangoes and cut each one into thick slices, on either side of the thin central stone. Put the slices on the griddle and cook for 5 minutes on each side.

Arrange the mangoes on serving plates and serve with lime wedges, to be squeezed over just before eating. Decorate with lime rind and serve with a dollop of Greek yogurt, if liked.

NUTRITIONAL INFORMATION Mangoes are a rich source of Vitamin A, and have good amounts of vitamins B and C. They have more carotenoids than most other fruit – these help keep colds at bay and can reduce the risk of cancer and heart disease. Mangoes also contain calcium, iron, potassium and protein.

115 kcals (483 kj) ■ **low fat** ■ **low GI** ■ **source of antioxidants** ■ **source of vitamins A, B and C**

218 Griddled pineapple and ginger

Preparation time:
5 minutes

Cooking time:
2–4 minutes

Serves: **4**

2 tablespoons icing sugar
1 teaspoon ground ginger
1 pineapple, peeled, cored and cut into
** 2.5 cm (1 inch) thick rounds**
4 tablespoons low-fat fromage frais,
** to serve**

Heat a griddle or a heavy-based frying pan.

Mix together the icing sugar and ginger and sprinkle over both sides of the pineapple rings. Put the pineapple on the griddle and cook for 1–2 minutes on each side until golden.

Serve the pineapple hot with the fromage frais.

91 kcals (383 kj) ■ **low fat** ■ **low GI** ■ **source of antioxidants** ■ **source of calcium**

219 Seasonal berries

220 Tropical fruit salad

Preparation time:
10 minutes, plus standing

Cooking time.
5 minutes

Serves: 4

250 g (8 oz) blackcurrants
500 g (1 lb) strawberries, hulled and
quartered or halved, according to size
500 g (1 lb) raspberries
250 g (8 oz) blackberries
250 g (8 oz) loganberries
300 ml (½ pint) rosé wine
½ teaspoon ground allspice

Gently mix together all the fruit in a large serving bowl.

Pour the wine into a saucepan and heat to boiling point. Add the allspice and immediately pour the hot wine over the fruit.

Allow the fruit to cool, then cover the bowl and leave to stand at room temperature for 4–6 hours before serving.

Preparation time:
15 minutes, plus chilling

Cooking time:
7 minutes

Serves: 4–6

2 kiwifruit, peeled and sliced
1 star fruit, sliced
2 mangoes, peeled, stoned and cubed
1 small papaya, deseeded, peeled and
cubed
6 lychees, peeled
1 banana, sliced
shredded rind of 1 lime, to decorate

DRESSING·
25 g (1 oz) sugar
100 ml (3½ fl oz) water
2 tablespoons lime juice
pulp and seeds of 2 passion fruit

First, to make the dressing, put the sugar and measurement water into a saucepan and heat until the sugar has dissolved. Add the lime juice and simmer for 5 minutes. Remove the pan from the heat and allow to cool. When the dressing is cool, stir in the passion fruit pulp and seeds.

Gently mix together all the prepared fruit in a large bowl. Pour the dressing over the fruit and chill for 15 minutes. Serve decorated with lime rind shreds.

NUTRITIONAL INFORMATION Kiwifruit are high in vitamin C – about the same as that of oranges, weight for weight. Fruits have varying contents of vitamin C, with blackcurrants and guavas among the highest, and plums and grapes among the lowest.

167 kcals (701 kj) ▪ **low fat** ▪ **low GI** ▪ **source of antioxidants** ▪ **source of vitamin C**

121 kcals (510 kj) ▪ **low fat** ▪ **low GI** ▪ **source of antioxidants** ▪ **source of vitamin C**

221 Papaya and lime salad

222 Bite-sized cappuccino meringues

Preparation time:
15 minutes

Cooking time:
5 minutes

Serves: **4**

3 firm ripe papayas
2 limes
2 teaspoons soft light brown sugar
50 g (2 oz) blanched almonds, toasted
lime wedges, to decorate

Cut the papayas in half, scoop out the seeds and discard. Peel the halves, cut the flesh roughly into dice and put into a bowl. Finely grate the rind of both limes, then squeeze one of the limes and reserve the juice. Remove the pith from the second lime. Working over the bowl of papaya to catch the juice, cut between the membranes to remove the segments. Add the lime segments and grated rind to the papaya.

Pour the reserved lime juice into a small saucepan with the sugar and heat gently until the sugar has dissolved. Remove from the heat and allow to cool. When the sweetened lime juice has cooled, pour it over the fruit and toss thoroughly. Add the toasted almonds to the fruit salad and decorate with lime wedges.

Preparation time:
15 minutes

Cooking time:
20–25 minutes

Oven temperature:
180°C (350°F) Gas Mark 4

Makes: **12**

3 small egg whites
175 g (6 oz) caster sugar
1 teaspoon strong black coffee or coffee
and chicory essence
250 g (8 oz) low-fat fromage frais
cocoa powder, to decorate (optional)
fanned strawberries, to serve

Whisk the egg whites in a large bowl until they are stiff. Fold in 1 tablespoon of the sugar and then gradually whisk in the remainder. The meringue must be glossy and form peaks when spoonfuls are dropped back into the bowl. Fold in the coffee or coffee essence.

Drop spoonfuls of the meringue on to a baking sheet lined with baking paper. Cook in a preheated oven, 180°C (350°F), Gas Mark 4, for 20–25 minutes, or until the meringues are golden and crisp. Remove from the oven and allow to cool for at least 10 minutes, then peel off the paper. Repeat with the remaining meringue mixture to make 24 little meringues in all.

Sandwich the meringues together in pairs with the fromage frais and serve immediately with strawberries. Dust with cocoa powder, if liked.

NUTRITIONAL INFORMATION There is very little nutritional difference between white and brown sugars. Brown sugar contains small traces of some minerals, but its main function in the diet, as with all sugars, is to add a pleasant sweetness to food.

151 kcals (632 kj) ■ low fat ■ low GI ■ source of antioxidants ■ source of vitamin C

70 kcals (295 kj) ■ low fat ■ source of calcium ■ source of vitamin C

223 Mango and pineapple pavlova

224 Hazelnut meringues with raspberries

Preparation time: **20 minutes**	**3 egg whites** **175 g (6 oz) caster sugar** **1 teaspoon strong black coffee**
Cooking time: **1 hour**	**250 g (8 oz) low-fat fromage frais** **125 g (4 oz) mango, peeled, stoned** **and diced**
Oven temperature: **120°C (250°F) Gas Mark ½**	**125 g (4 oz) fresh pineapple, peeled,** **cored and cut into chunks** **pulp and seeds of 1–2 passion fruits**
Serves: **4**	

Whisk the egg whites in a large bowl until they are stiff. Fold in 1 tablespoon of the sugar and then gradually whisk in the remainder. The meringue must be glossy and form peaks when spoonfuls are dropped back into the bowl. Fold in the coffee.

Spread the meringue mixture over a large sheet of baking paper to form a 20 cm (8 inch) diameter round. Make a slight hollow in the centre of the meringue and cook in a preheated oven, 120°C (250°F), Gas Mark ½, for 1 hour until the meringue is crisp. Remove from the oven and allow to cool for about 10 minutes, then peel off the paper.

When the meringue is cold, fill the hollow in the top with fromage frais. Arrange the mango and pineapple on top, then drizzle the passion fruit pulp and seeds over the fruit.

Preparation time: **15 minutes**	**2 egg whites** **125 g (4 oz) icing sugar, sifted, plus extra** **to decorate (optional)**
Cooking time: **15–20 minutes**	**50 g (2 oz) hazelnuts, finely chopped** **500 g (1 lb) raspberries** **mint leaves, to decorate**
Oven temperature: **180°C (350°F) Gas Mark 4**	
Serves: **6**	

Whisk the egg whites in a large bowl until they are stiff. Fold in 1 tablespoon of the sugar and then gradually whisk in the remainder. Continue to whisk until very thick. Carefully fold in the hazelnuts. Pipe the meringue mixture on to a nonstick baking sheet in swirls.

Bake the meringues in a preheated oven, 180°C (350°F), Gas Mark 4, for 15–20 minutes. Allow to cool slightly, then transfer to a wire rack to cool completely.

Serve the meringues with the raspberries and decorate with mint leaves. Dust with icing sugar, if liked.

NUTRITIONAL INFORMATION Meringues and pavlovas are fantastic desserts for anyone with a sweet tooth who is also watching their weight – especially when using fromage frais or Greek yogurt instead of cream.

243 kcals (1021 kj) ■ low fat ■ source of antioxidants

160 kcals (680 kj) ■ low fat ■ source of antioxidants ■ source of vitamin C

Preparation time:
10 minutes

Serves: **4**

6 ginger biscuits, lightly crushed
200 g (7 oz) low-fat cream cheese
200 g (7 oz) low-fat fromage frais
few drops of vanilla extract
1 tablespoon caster sugar
grated rind and juice of 1 lime
125 g (4 oz) raspberries
lime wedges, to decorate

Divide the biscuits between 4 small glass dishes.

Mix together the cream cheese, fromage frais, vanilla extract, sugar and lime rind and juice in a bowl.

Spoon the mixture on to the biscuits, then top with the raspberries. Serve immediately, decorated with a lime wedge.

Preparation time:
30 minutes, plus chilling

Cooking time:
about 1 hour

Oven temperature:
190°C (375°F) Gas Mark 5

Serves: **10**

500 g (1 lb) skimmed ricotta cheese
2 large eggs
75 g (3 oz) granulated sugar
150 ml (¼ pint) low-fat natural yogurt
4 tablespoons lemon juice
grated rind of 2 lemons
2 tablespoons plain flour
2 teaspoons vanilla extract
2 egg whites
150 g (5 oz) low-fat fromage frais
300 g (10 oz) fresh blueberries

CRUST:
125 g (4 oz) digestive biscuits, crushed
2 tablespoons sugar
1 teaspoon ground cinnamon
15 g (½ oz) unsaturated spread
1 egg white

To make the crust, mix together the biscuits, sugar, cinnamon and spread in a bowl. In a separate bowl, whisk the egg white until frothy. Stir the egg white into the crumb mixture. Press the crust into a 23 cm (9 inch) springform tin and bake in a preheated oven, 190°C (375°F), Gas Mark 5, for 7–10 minutes until lightly browned. Allow to cool.

To make the filling, whiz the ricotta and eggs in a food processor until smooth. Beat together the cheese mixture, sugar, yogurt, lemon juice and rind, flour and vanilla extract. In another bowl, beat the egg whites until soft peaks form, then fold into the cheese mixture. Spread over the crust. Bake in the oven for 50–55 minutes until firm to the touch.

Loosen the edge of the cheesecake. Allow the cheesecake to cool. Remove the sides of the tin, cover the cheesecake and refrigerate for up to 1 day. Decorate with fromage frais and blueberries, and serve.

180 kcals (754 kj) ▪ **low fat** ▪ **source of antioxidants** ▪ **source of calcium**

177 kcals (744 kj) ▪ **low fat** ▪ **source of antioxidants** ▪ **source of calcium**

227 Frozen strawberry yogurt

228 Cranberry ice

Preparation time:
15 minutes, plus freezing

Cooking time:
about 5 minutes

Serves: **3**

250 g (8 oz) strawberries, roughly chopped
2 tablespoons red grape juice
1 tablespoon crème de cassis
2 tablespoons icing sugar
300 ml (½ pint) low-fat natural yogurt

Put the strawberries into a saucepan. Add the grape juice and warm gently, stirring occasionally, until the strawberries become soft and pulpy. Press the strawberries through a nylon sieve, reserving the juice in a large bowl. Discard the seeds. Beat in the crème de cassis, icing sugar and yogurt.

Pour the mixture into an ice-cream machine and churn until the mixture becomes thick and frozen. If you don't have an ice-cream machine, transfer the mixture to a shallow freezer container. Freeze for at least 1 hour, or until the mixture is just beginning to set around the edges. Remove the container from the freezer and beat the mixture until smooth, then return it to the freezer. Freeze for a further 30 minutes, then beat again. Repeat the freezing and beating process several more times until the yogurt is completely frozen.

The yogurt can be stored in the freezer for up to 2 weeks. Transfer it from the freezer to the refrigerator 20 minutes before serving.

Preparation time:
10 minutes, plus cooling and freezing

Cooking time:
10 minutes

Serves: **4**

375 ml (13 fl oz) cranberry juice
90 g (3½ oz) caster sugar
125 g (4 oz) cranberries, defrosted if frozen
3 tablespoons finely grated orange rind

TO DECORATE:
mint sprigs
sugar-frosted cranberries (see Cook's Notes, below)

Put the cranberry juice and sugar into a saucepan and heat gently until the sugar has dissolved. Bring to the boil and simmer for 5 minutes. Remove the pan from the heat, stir in the cranberries and orange rind and allow the mixture to cool completely.

Pour the mixture into an ice-cream machine and churn until the mixture becomes thick and frozen. If you don't have an ice-cream machine, transfer the mixture to a shallow freezer container. Freeze for at least 1 hour, or until the mixture is just beginning to set around the edges. Remove the container from the freezer and beat the mixture until smooth, then return it to the freezer. Freeze for a further 30 minutes, then beat again. Repeat the freezing and beating process several more times until the mixture is completely frozen.

Transfer the cranberry ice from the freezer to the refrigerator 15 minutes before serving and scoop it into individual bowls. Decorate with mint sprigs and sugar-frosted cranberries.

COOK'S NOTES To make sugar-frosted cranberries, dip washed and dried cranberries into lightly beaten egg white, then roll them in caster sugar. Set aside on kitchen paper to dry.

134 kcals (558 kj) ■ **low fat** ■ **low GI** ■ **source of antioxidants** ■ **source of vitamin C**

236 kcals (984 kj) ■ **low fat** ■ **source of antioxidants** ■ **source of vitamin C**

229 Papaya and lime sorbet

Preparation time:
30 minutes, plus cooling and freezing

Cooking time:
10 minutes

Serves: **4**

150 ml (¼ pint) cold water
125 g (4 oz) granulated sugar
1 ripe papaya, about 500 g (1 lb), deseeded, peeled and diced
juice and grated rind of 2 limes
lime wedges, to decorate

Put the measurement water and sugar into a saucepan and heat gently until the sugar has dissolved. Bring to the boil and boil for 5 minutes. Remove the pan from the heat and allow to cool.

Set aside 2 tablespoons of the diced papaya and whiz the remainder in a food processor or blender with the cooled sugar syrup until smooth.

Stir the lime juice and grated rind into the papaya purée, then pour into a shallow freezer container. Freeze for 3 hours.

Remove the sorbet from the freezer and beat with a fork to break up the ice crystals. Stir in the reserved diced papaya, return to the freezer and freeze until solid.

Remove the sorbet from the freezer 10 minutes before serving. Serve with lime wedges.

230 Summer berry sorbet

Preparation time:
5 minutes, plus freezing

Serves: **2**

250 g (8 oz) frozen mixed summer berries
75 ml (3 fl oz) spiced berry cordial
2 tablespoons kirsch or vodka
1 tablespoon fresh lime juice

Chill a shallow freezer container. Put the berries, cordial, kirsch or vodka and lime juice into a food processor or blender and whiz until smooth. Do not over-process, as this will soften the mixture too much.

Turn the purée into the chilled container and freeze for at least 25 minutes. Spoon the sorbet into bowls and serve immediately.

NUTRITIONAL INFORMATION This colourful mixed summer berry sorbet is very refreshing and bursting with vitamin C.

164 kcals (684 kj) ■ **low fat** ■ **source of vitamin C**

106 kcals (443 kj) ■ **low fat** ■ **source of antioxidants** ■ **source of vitamin C**

Preparation time:
15 minutes, plus cooling, standing and freezing

Cooking time:
15 minutes

Serves: **6**

600 ml (1 pint) water, plus 3 tablespoons
250 g (8 oz) granulated sugar
3 teaspoons powdered gelatine
rind of 2 lemons
300 ml (½ pint) fresh lemon juice
2 egg whites
candied lemon peel, to serve (optional)

Put the 600 ml (1 pint) water and sugar into a small saucepan and heat gently until the sugar dissolves. Bring to the boil and boil for 10 minutes. Remove the pan from the heat and allow to cool.

Put the 3 tablespoons water into a small heatproof bowl and sprinkle over the gelatine. Set the bowl over a saucepan of simmering water and leave until the gelatine goes spongy. Whisk the gelatine mixture into the syrup with the lemon rind and juice.

Pour the lemon mixture into a freezer container and freeze for about 1 hour until partially frozen. Turn the partially frozen mixture into a chilled bowl and beat lightly with a fork to break up the ice crystals.

Whisk the egg whites in a large bowl until they are stiff. Carefully fold into the lemon mixture. Freeze for a further 1½ hours, then whisk again and freeze until firm. Decorate with candied lemon peel, if liked.

Preparation time:
10 minutes, plus cooling and freezing

Serves: **4**

4 tablespoons freshly ground strong coffee
125 g (4 oz) caster sugar
450 ml (¾ pint) boiling water

Put the coffee and sugar into a jug and stir in the measurement water. Stir until the sugar has dissolved, then allow to cool.

Strain the coffee liquid into a freezer container and chill in the refrigerator for about 30 minutes. Transfer the mixture to the freezer and freeze for at least 2 hours, or until completely solid.

Remove the granita from the container, then quickly chop it into large chunks with a large strong knife. Return it to the container and freeze again until required. Serve straight from the freezer.

COOK'S NOTES If you are using an ice-cream machine to make this sorbet, follow the recipe until the end of the second step. Pour the mixture into the machine and churn until half frozen. Whisk the egg whites until they form soft peaks and add to the half-frozen mixture. Churn again until completely frozen. Decorate with candied lemon peel.

172 kcals (717 kj) ■ **low fat** ■ **source of vitamin C**

123 kcals (515 kj) ■ **low fat**

233 Strawberry jellies

234 Red berry terrine

Preparation time:
10 minutes, plus standing and chilling

Cooking time:
5 minutes

Serves: **6**

450 g (14½ oz) strawberries, hulled
300 ml (½ pint) boiling water
100 g (3½ oz) caster sugar
500 ml (17 fl oz) white grape juice
2 x 12 g (½ oz) sachets powdered gelatine
 or 6 leaves
75 ml (3 fl oz) crème de cassis (optional)

Preparation time:
10 minutes, plus standing and chilling

Cooking time:
5 minutes

Serves: **6**

450 ml (¾ pint) unsweetened red grape
 juice
2 x 12 g (½ oz) sachets powdered gelatine
50 g (2 oz) caster sugar
500 g (1 lb) bag frozen mixed berry fruits

Roughly chop three-quarters of the strawberries and put into a food processor or blender with the measurement water and the sugar and whiz until smooth. Transfer the mixture to a sieve set over a bowl and stir to allow the liquid to drip through.

Pour 200 ml (7 fl oz) of the grape juice into a small heatproof bowl and sprinkle over the gelatine, making sure that all the powder has been absorbed by the juice. Allow to stand for 10 minutes.

Set the bowl over a saucepan of simmering water and stir until the gelatine has completely dissolved. Leave to cool, then stir in the crème de cassis, if using, strawberry liquid and the remaining grape juice.

Arrange the remaining strawberries in 6 large wine glasses, pour over the liquid and chill until the jelly has set.

Pour 150 ml (¼ pint) of the grape juice into a heatproof bowl and sprinkle over the gelatine, making sure that all the powder has been absorbed by the juice. Allow to stand for 10 minutes.

Set the bowl over a saucepan of simmering water and stir until the gelatine has completely dissolved.

Stir the sugar into the gelatine mixture, then mix with the remaining grape juice.

Pour the still-frozen fruits into a 1 kg (2 lb) loaf tin, then cover with the warm juice mixture. Mix together, then chill in the refrigerator for 3 hours until set and the fruits have defrosted completely.

To serve, dip the loaf tin into a bowl of just-boiled water. Count to 10, then loosen the edge of the jelly and turn out on to a serving plate. Serve the jelly cut into thick slices.

124 kcals (519 kj) ■ **low fat** ■ **source of vitamin C**

108 kcals (452 kj) ■ **low fat** ■ **low GI** ■ **source of antioxidants** ■ **source of vitamin C**

235 Apple and fig crumble

Preparation time:	**125 g (4 oz) plain wholemeal flour**
20 minutes	**50 g (2 oz) unsaturated spread, cut into pieces**
Cooking time:	**50 g (2 oz) soft brown sugar**
25–30 minutes	**500 g (1 lb) cooking apples, such as Bramleys, peeled, cored and sliced**
Oven temperature:	**6 dried or fresh figs, diced**
180°C (350°F) Gas Mark 4	**grated rind and juice of 1 lemon**
	1 teaspoon ground cinnamon
Serves: **6**	

Sift the flour into a large bowl, add the saturated spread and rub in with the fingertips until the mixture resembles coarse crumbs. Stir in the sugar.

Put the fruit into a 1.2 litre (2 pint) ovenproof dish. Add the lemon rind and juice and cinnamon. Spoon the crumble mixture over the fruit and bake in a preheated oven, 180°C (350°F), Gas Mark 4, for 25–30 minutes until golden brown. Serve warm.

NUTRITIONAL INFORMATION Figs are high in dietary fibre, low in fat and offer a non-dairy source of calcium, iron and magnesium. They are ideal ingredients in baking, salads and snacks.

222 kcals (929 kj) ■ low fat ■ high fibre ■ source of calcium ■ source of iron ■ source of magnesium

236 Bread pudding

Preparation time:	**250 g (8 oz) stale bread, cut into chunks**
15 minutes, plus soaking	**250 g (8 oz) dried mixed fruit**
	50 g (2 oz) mixed candied peel (optional)
Cooking time:	**75 g (3 oz) soft brown sugar**
1½–1¾ hours	**¼ teaspoon ground mixed spice**
	50 g (2 oz) unsalted butter, plus extra for greasing
Oven temperature:	
160°C (325°F) Gas Mark 3	**2 tablespoons marmalade**
	2 eggs, beaten
Serves: **6**	**1–2 tablespoons caster sugar**

Put the bread into a large bowl, cover with cold water and leave to soak for about 20 minutes.

Drain the bread and squeeze it to remove as much water as possible. Return it to the bowl and beat well with a fork. Stir in the fruit, mixed candied peel, if using, brown sugar and mixed spice.

Put the butter and marmalade into a saucepan and heat gently until melted. Take care not to over-heat. Pour the butter and marmalade mixture on to the eggs, mix well and stir into the bread mixture. Pour into a greased ovenproof dish, sprinkle with the caster sugar and bake in a preheated oven, 160°C (325°F), Gas Mark 3, for 1½–1¾ hours until golden brown and firm. Serve hot or cold, cut into slices.

NUTRITIONAL INFORMATION Use a wholegrain seeded bread to increase the fibre content of this recipe, and to add a nutty texture.

373 kcals (1557 kj) ■ low fat ■ source of potassium

10 Baking

237 Apple and apricot muffins

Preparation time:
20 minutes

Cooking time:
15–20 minutes

Oven temperature:
200°C (400°F) Gas Mark 6

Makes: **12**

100 g (3½ oz) plain wholemeal flour
150 g (5 oz) plain flour
1 teaspoon baking powder
1 teaspoon bicarbonate of soda
2 tablespoons golden caster sugar
100 g (3½ oz) ready-to-eat dried apricots,
** chopped**
½ teaspoon ground cinnamon
2 red dessert apples, peeled, cored and
** chopped**
1 egg, beaten
50 g (2 oz) margarine, melted
200 ml (7 fl oz) semi-skimmed milk

Line a 12-section muffin tin with paper muffin cases. Sift the flours, baking powder and bicarbonate of soda into a large bowl, tipping any bran in the sieve back into the bowl. Stir in the sugar, apricots, cinnamon and apples.

In a separate bowl, whisk together all the remaining ingredients, then gently stir them into the flour mixture, making sure that you don't beat too much, as this will spoil the end result.

Spoon the mixture into the muffin cases and bake in a preheated oven, 200°C (400°F), Gas Mark 6, for 15–20 minutes. Allow to cool a little before serving.

NUTRITIONAL INFORMATION Choose a margarine without hydrogenated oils. Hydrogenated oils are often used in margarines to solidify oil. This creates trans fats, which act like saturated fat in the body, increasing cholesterol and the risk of heart disease.

141 kcals (592 kj) ■ **low fat** ■ **high fibre** ■ **source of calcium** ■ **source of vitamin C**

238 Peanut butter and banana biscuits

Preparation time:
15 minutes

Cooking time:
10–15 minutes

Oven temperature:
190°C (375°F) Gas Mark 5

Makes: **about 28**

125 g (4 oz) butter, softened
150 g (5 oz) caster sugar
1 egg, beaten
1 teaspoon baking powder
125 g (4 oz) crunchy peanut butter
150 g (5 oz) plain flour
100 g (3½ oz) dried banana chunks,
** roughly chopped**
about 28 unsalted peanuts

Put the butter, sugar, egg, baking powder, peanut butter and flour into a food processor or blender and whiz until well mixed. Stir in the banana chunks. Roll the dough into balls about the size of a walnut and put on lightly greased baking sheets, allowing enough space for the mixture to spread as it bakes. Using the palm of your hand, flatten the balls slightly.

Press a whole peanut into the middle of each biscuit and bake in a preheated oven, 190°C (375°F), Gas Mark 5, for 10–15 minutes, or until the biscuits are just beginning to brown around the edges.

Remove the biscuits from the oven and allow to cool slightly. Using a palette knife, transfer them to a wire rack to cool completely. The biscuits can be stored in an airtight container for up to 5 days.

127 kcals (533 kj) ■ **low fat** ■ **low carb** ■ **high fibre** ■ **source of protein**

239 Carrot and orange muffins

240 Chocolate crunch crisps

Preparation time:
15 minutes

Cooking time:
15–20 minutes

Oven temperature:
200°C (400°F) Gas Mark 6

Makes: **6**

butter, for greasing (optional)
150 g (5 oz) self-raising flour
¼ teaspoon baking powder
75 g (3 oz) caster sugar
finely grated rind and juice of 1 orange
125 g (4 oz) carrots, coarsely grated
100 ml (3½ fl oz) semi-skimmed milk
2 eggs, beaten
2 tablespoons sunflower oil
1 tablespoon apricot jam, warmed, to serve

Line a 6-section muffin tin with paper muffin cases or grease the tins well. Sift the flour and baking powder into a large bowl and add the sugar, orange rind and grated carrot. Mix together and make a well in the centre.

In a separate bowl, mix together the milk, eggs, orange juice and oil. Pour the liquid ingredients into the dry ones and stir until just blended.

Fill the muffin cases or tins two-thirds full with the mixture. Bake in a preheated oven, 200°C (400°F), Gas Mark 6, for 15–20 minutes, or until a skewer inserted into the centre of a muffin comes out clean. Transfer the muffins to a wire rack to cool.

Brush the tops of the muffins with a little warmed apricot jam and serve immediately.

Preparation time:
5–10 minutes, plus chilling

Cooking time:
5 minutes

Makes: **20**

125 g (4 oz) margarine
2 tablespoons golden syrup
25 g (1 oz) cocoa powder
250 g (8 oz) puffed rice or millet
125 g (4 oz) ready-to-eat dried cranberries or raisins

Put the margarine and syrup into a large heavy-based saucepan and heat, stirring, until the margarine has melted.

Add a little of the syrup mixture to the cocoa powder and mix to form a smooth paste, then return the paste to the saucepan and blend well. Add the puffed rice or millet and cranberries or raisins and stir carefully until evenly coated.

Divide the mixture between 20 paper sweet cases and chill the crisps in the refrigerator until set.

224 kcals (942 kj) ■ low fat ■ source of antioxidants ■ source of vitamin C

127 kcals (532 kj) ■ low fat ■ source of potassium

241 Cranberry and sunflower seed biscuits

242 Millet and cranberry flapjacks

Preparation time: **15 minutes**	**4 tablespoons sunflower seeds**
	2 tablespoons sunflower oil, plus extra for oiling
Cooking time: **13 minutes**	**75 g (3 oz) margarine**
	125 g (4 oz) light muscovado sugar
	1 egg
Oven temperature: **180°C (350°F) Gas Mark 4**	**100 g (3½ oz) self-raising white flour**
	75 g (3 oz) self-raising wholemeal flour
	grated rind of ½ small orange
Makes: **about 25**	**75 g (3 oz) ready-to-eat dried cranberries**

Preparation time: **10 minutes**	**125 g (4 oz) margarine, plus extra for greasing**
	50 g (2 oz) unrefined demerara or raw cane light brown sugar
Cooking time: **35 minutes**	**2 tablespoons golden syrup**
	250 g (8 oz) millet flakes or rolled oats
Oven temperature: **180°C (350°F) Gas Mark 4**	**1 tablespoon ready-to-eat dried cranberries**
Makes: **16**	

Heat a nonstick frying pan and dry-fry the sunflower seeds, stirring constantly, for 2–3 minutes until golden. Grind to a fine paste with the oil, using a spice grinder, clean coffee grinder or a pestle and mortar.

Cream the margarine and sugar in a bowl. Gradually beat in the egg, then mix in the flours. Mix in the sunflower paste, then stir in the orange rind and cranberries.

Drop heaped teaspoonfuls of the mixture on to lightly oiled baking sheets, spacing them well apart. Bake in a preheated oven,180°C (350°F), Gas Mark 4, for 10 minutes until golden. Leave on the baking sheets to firm up for a few minutes, then transfer to a wire rack to cool.

Put the margarine, sugar and syrup into a saucepan and gently heat until melted. Remove the pan from the heat and add the millet flakes or rolled oats and dried cranberries, mixing thoroughly.

Grease a 20 cm (8 inch) square sandwich tin. Spoon the flapjack mixture into the tin and level with a palette knife. Bake in a preheated oven, 180°C (350°F), Gas Mark 4, for 30 minutes, or until golden brown.

Leave the flapjacks to cool in the tin for 5 minutes, then mark them into 16 portions. Allow to cool completely, then remove the flapjacks from the tin. Store in an airtight container until required.

NUTRITIONAL INFORMATION Sunflower seeds are a good source of protein and vitamin E. They are also high in linoleic acid – needed for the maintenance of cell membranes.

74 kcals (308 kj) ▪ low fat ▪ low carb ▪ source of potassium ▪ source of protein ▪ source of vitamin E

147 kcals (618 kj) ▪ low fat ▪ high fibre

243 Scones

244 Moist beetroot cake

Preparation time: **12 minutes**	**250 g (8 oz) plain white or wholemeal flour, plus extra for dusting** **½ teaspoon salt**
Cooking time: **7–10 minutes**	**4 teaspoons baking powder** **25–50 g (1–2 oz) margarine, diced** **150 ml (¼ pint) semi-skimmed milk**
Oven temperature: **230°C (450°F) Gas Mark 8**	**semi-skimmed milk or flour, to finish** TO SERVE:
Makes: **about 12**	**margarine, to spread** **raspberry or strawberry jam** **whipped cream (optional)**

Sift the flour, salt and baking powder into a large bowl, add the margarine and rub in with the fingertips until the mixture resembles fine breadcrumbs. Make a well in the centre, pour in the milk and mix to a soft spongy dough, adding a little water if necessary.

Turn out the dough on to a floured surface, and knead quickly and lightly. Roll out the dough with a floured rolling pin or flatten it with floured hands until it is 1.5 cm (¾ inch) thick. Cut into rounds using a 6 cm (2½ inch) floured pastry cutter or a tumbler. Put the scones on a greased baking sheet.

Shape the remaining dough into a ball, flatten into a circle, cut out more rounds and put on the baking sheet. Brush the scones with milk for a glazed finish or rub them with flour for a soft crust. Bake near the top of a preheated oven, 230°C (450°F), Gas Mark 8, for 7–10 minutes, until well risen and golden on top.

To serve, split the scones and spread with margarine, raspberry or strawberry jam and whipped cream, if liked.

Preparation time: **15 minutes**	**margarine, for greasing** **250 g (8 oz) self-raising flour** **½ teaspoon ground nutmeg**
Cooking time: **45 minutes**	**½ teaspoon ground mixed spice** **150 g (5 oz) light muscovado sugar** **½ ripe banana, mashed**
Oven temperature: **180°C (350°F) Gas Mark 4**	**250 g (8 oz) cooked beetroot, peeled and finely grated** **2 small eggs, beaten**
Makes: **12 squares**	**125 ml (4 fl oz) semi-skimmed milk** **250 g (8 oz) low-fat fromage frais**

Grease and line a 20 cm (8 inch) shallow square cake tin. Sift the flour and spices into a large bowl. Stir in the sugar, banana and all but 25 g (1 oz) of the beetroot. Make a well in the centre and add the eggs and milk. Beat well, then pour the mixture into the prepared cake tin.

Bake the cake in a preheated oven, 180°C (350°F), Gas Mark 4, for 45 minutes, or until a skewer inserted into the centre comes out clean. Allow to cool in the tin for about 10 minutes, then turn out on to a wire rack to cool completely.

Spread the fromage frais over the cake and scatter the remaining beetroot pieces on the top. Cut the cake into 12 squares and serve.

NUTRITIONAL INFORMATION Beetroot contains a high amount of antioxidants, in particular the pigment anthocyanin, which has anti-cancer properties. It also contains other beneficial vitamins and minerals including beta-carotene, vitamins B6 and C, folic acid, manganese, calcium, magnesium, iron, potassium and phosphorous.

92 kcals (386 kj) ■ low fat ■ low carb ■ source of calcium

155 kcals (652 kj) ■ low fat ■ source of antioxidants ■ source of potassium

245 Banana and raisin tea bread

246 Tea cakes

Preparation time: **10 minutes**	**75 g (3 oz) low-fat spread, plus a little extra for greasing** **150 g (5 oz) self-raising wholemeal flour**
Cooking time: **50 minutes–1 hour**	**75 g (3 oz) plain wholemeal flour** **1 teaspoon baking powder** **1 teaspoon ground cinnamon**
Oven temperature: **180°C (350°F) Gas Mark 4**	**75 g (3 oz) soft brown sugar** **3 bananas, well mashed** **100 g (3½ oz) seedless raisins**
Serves: **12**	**2 eggs, lightly beaten**

Grease a 1 kg (2 lb) loaf tin. Melt the spread in a small saucepan over a low heat. Sift the flours, baking powder and cinnamon into a large bowl. Stir in the sugar, mashed bananas, melted spread, raisins and eggs and beat for 3 minutes until smooth.

Turn the mixture into the prepared tin and bake in a preheated oven, 180°C (350°F), Gas Mark 4, for 50 minutes–1 hour or until a skewer inserted into the centre comes out clean. Stand the tin on a wire rack to cool slightly before turning out.

Preparation time: **25 minutes, plus proving and rising**	**500 g (1 lb) plain flour** **1 teaspoon salt** **2 teaspoons sugar, plus extra for creaming the yeast**
Cooking time: **20–22 minutes**	**100 g (3½ oz) currants** **25 g (1 oz) fresh yeast**

Oven temperature:
220°C (425°F) Gas Mark 7
	**300 ml (½ pint) semi-skimmed milk,
	    warmed**
	**low-fat spread, melted for greasing and
	    brushing, and to serve**

Makes: **8**	

Sift the flour and salt into a large bowl and stir in the sugar and currants. Cream the yeast with a little extra sugar and some of the warm milk. Pour the yeast mixture into a well in the centre of the flour and leave in a warm place for 10 minutes.

Add the remaining milk to the yeast mixture, mix to a light dough and knead well. Cover the bowl with polythene or a clean tea towel and leave in a warm place to rise for about 1–1½ hours until doubled in size.

Knead the dough again, then divide it into 8 pieces and roll and shape them into round tea cakes. Prick each one with a fork. Put the tea cakes on a greased baking sheet, cover with a tea towel and leave to rise in a warm place for 30 minutes.

Bake the tea cakes in a preheated oven, 220°C (425°F), Gas Mark 7, for 10–12 minutes. Remove them from the oven and brush with melted low-fat spread, then return to the oven for a further 10 minutes.

To serve, split each tea cake in half, toast lightly and spread with low-fat spread.

190 kcals (798 kj) ▪ **low fat** ▪ **high fibre** ▪ **source of potassium**

276 kcals (1154 kj) ▪ **low fat** ▪ **source of calcium** ▪ **source of potassium**

247 Bara brith

248 Pesto twists

Preparation time:	250 ml (8 fl oz) strong cold tea
10 minutes, plus soaking	4 tablespoons marmalade
	175 g (6 oz) seedless sultanas
Cooking time:	200 g (7 oz) golden granulated sugar
2 hours	300 g (10 oz) self-raising flour
	2 eggs, beaten
Oven temperature:	good pinch of ground mixed spice
150°C (300°F) Gas Mark 2	margarine, for greasing

Serves: **12**

Put the cold tea into a bowl with the marmalade and sultanas. Leave to soak for 1 hour.

Stir the sugar, flour and eggs into the tea mixture, add the mixed spice and mix well. Spoon the mixture into a greased 1 kg (2 lb) loaf tin and cook in a preheated oven, 150°C (300°F), Gas Mark 2, for 2 hours, or until a skewer inserted into the centre comes out clean.

NUTRITIONAL INFORMATION Dried fruit such as currants, sultanas, raisins, dates and figs provide energy in the form of sugar and are also a good source of fibre.

192 kcals (805 kj) ■ low fat ■ source of antioxidants ■ source of potassium

Preparation time:	250 g (8 oz) strong plain flour, plus extra
25 minutes, plus rising	for dusting
	½ teaspoon salt
Cooking time:	1 teaspoon fast-action dried yeast
15 minutes	150 ml (¼ pint) warm water
	handful of basil leaves
Oven temperature:	1 teaspoon pine nuts
220°C (425°F) Gas Mark 7	1 teaspoon freshly grated Parmesan
	cheese

Makes: **8**

Sift the flour into a large bowl, then add the salt and yeast. Pour the measurement water into a food processor or blender and add the basil, pine nuts and Parmesan. Whiz for a few seconds to form a runny paste.

Make a well in the centre of the flour and stir in the basil paste, bringing the mixture together with a round-bladed knife. The dough will be quite wet, so turn it out on to a well-floured surface and knead for 10 minutes, or until the dough is soft and elastic. Put the dough into a clean bowl. Cover with a damp tea towel and leave to rise in a warm place for 1 hour, or until doubled in size.

Tip out the dough on to a floured surface and knock back. (Knocking back means kneading with your knuckles to knock out the air bubbles and produce a more even texture.) Knead for 5 minutes. Divide the dough into 8 pieces. Roll each piece into a long thin sausage shape. Tie each sausage into a knot and put on a nonstick baking sheet. Cover the twists with a damp tea towel and leave to rise for 1 hour, or until doubled in size again.

Bake the twists in a preheated oven, 220°C (425°F), Gas Mark 7, for 15 minutes, or until they sound hollow when tapped on the base.

114 kcals (480 kj) ■ low fat ■ source of calcium

249 Five-seed rolls

250 Rice and rye bread

Preparation time:
20 minutes, plus rising

Cooking time:
15 minutes

Oven temperature:
220°C (425°F) Gas Mark 7

Makes: **8**

250 g (8 oz) strong plain flour, plus extra for dusting
1 teaspoon salt
1 teaspoon fast-action dried yeast
1 teaspoon sunflower seeds
1 teaspoon poppy seeds
1 teaspoon pumpkin seeds
1 teaspoon sesame seeds
1 teaspoon cumin seeds
150–200 ml (¼ pint–7 fl oz) semi-skimmed milk, warmed

Preparation time:
20 minutes, plus proving and rising

Cooking time:
40–50 minutes

Oven temperature:
200°C (400°F) Gas Mark 6

Serves: **8**

300 ml (½ pint) tepid water
1 teaspoon sugar
15 g (½ oz) fast-action dried yeast
175 g (6 oz) brown rice flour
175 g (6 oz) rye flour
1 teaspoon salt
25 ml (1 fl oz) sunflower oil
margarine, for greasing
1 tablespoon coriander seeds (optional)
½ tablespoon cumin seeds (optional)

Sift the flour into a large bowl. Stir in the salt and the yeast, then stir in the seeds.

Make a well in the centre of the flour and stir in the warm milk. Bring the mixture together, then knead well on a lightly floured surface for 10 minutes, or until the dough is smooth and elastic. Put into a clean bowl. Cover with a damp tea towel and leave to rise in a warm place for 1 hour, or until the dough has doubled in size.

Tip out the dough on to a floured surface and knock back (see recipe 248). Divide the dough into 8 pieces and shape into rolls. Transfer to a nonstick baking sheet. Cover with a damp tea towel and leave to rise in a warm place for 1 hour, or until the dough has doubled in size again.

Bake the rolls in a preheated oven, 220°C (425°F) Gas Mark 7, for 10 minutes. Dust the part-baked rolls with flour and return them to the oven for another 5 minutes. The rolls are cooked when they are evenly browned and sound hollow when tapped on the base.

Put the measurement water into a small bowl, add the sugar and stir until it has dissolved. Sprinkle the yeast on the top and leave in a warm place until it begins to froth.

Sift the flours and salt into a large bowl, then add the oil and the yeast mixture. Beat to a thick pouring consistency.

Put the bread mixture into a greased 500 g (1 lb) loaf tin and seal inside a large polythene bag. Leave the dough to rise in a warm place for about 1 hour, or until it has doubled in size. Remove from the polythene bag and sprinkle the top of the dough with the coriander and cumin seeds, if using.

Bake the bread in a preheated oven, 200°C (400°F), Gas Mark 6, for 25–30 minutes. Remove the partially baked bread from the tin and put on a baking sheet. Bake for a further 15–20 minutes to make a nice crust.

NUTRITIONAL INFORMATION Brown rice flour is very high in fibre and can be used instead of plain or wholemeal flour in soups and casseroles as a thickener.

126 kcals (527 kj) ▪ low fat ▪ low GI ▪ source of phytoestrogens

181 kcals (755 kj) ▪ low fat ▪ low GI ▪ high fibre

251 Soft wholemeal rolls

252 Olive bread rolls

Preparation time:
30 minutes, plus proving and rising

Cooking time:
15–20 minutes

Oven temperature:
230°C (450°) Gas Mark 8

Makes: **8**

250 g (8 oz) plain wholemeal flour, plus extra for dusting
1 teaspoon salt
25 g (1 oz) low-fat spread, cut into pieces
15 g (½ oz) fresh yeast or 1½ teaspoons fast-action dried yeast with 1 teaspoon sugar
about 150 ml (¼ pint) semi-skimmed milk, warmed
vegetable oil, for oiling

Preparation time:
30–45 minutes, plus proving and rising

Cooking time:
20–25 minutes

Oven temperature:
220°C (425°F) Gas Mark 7

Makes: **8**

2½ teaspoons fast-action dried yeast
300 ml (½ pint) warm water
1 teaspoon caster sugar
500 g (1 lb) strong plain white flour, plus extra for dusting
125 g (4 oz) plain wholemeal flour
2 teaspoons each dried mint and oregano
1½ teaspoons salt, plus extra to sprinkle
3 tablespoons olive oil, plus extra for oiling and drizzling
175 g (6 oz) Kalamata olives, pitted

Sift the flour and salt into a large bowl and warm gently. Add the low-fat spread and rub in with the fingertips. Blend the fresh yeast with the warm milk and leave for 10 minutes to froth. If using dried yeast, sprinkle into the milk and leave for 15–20 minutes until frothy.

Pour the yeast liquid into the flour and mix, adding a little more milk if necessary. Beat until the dough leaves the sides of the bowl clean, then turn out on to a floured surface and knead for 10 minutes. Transfer the dough into an oiled polythene bag and leave to rise until doubled in size.

Tip out the dough on to a floured surface and knock back (see recipe 248). Form into a fat sausage shape and cut across into 8 equal-sized pieces. Shape into rounds or ovals and press down firmly with the heel of your hand. Put the rolls on a floured baking sheet, leaving room for them to expand. Cover and leave to rise for 15 minutes, or until doubled in size.

Dust the rolls with flour and bake in the centre of a preheated oven, 230°C (450°), Gas Mark 8, for 15–20 minutes. Transfer to a wire rack, cover with a tea towel and allow to cool a little before serving

Dissolve the yeast in the measurement water, stir in the sugar and leave in a warm place for 10 minutes until it begins to froth.

Sift the flours into a food mixer and stir in the herbs and salt. Gradually work in the frothy yeast mixture and the oil to form a soft dough, adding a little extra warm water if necessary. Knead for 8–10 minutes until the dough is smooth and elastic.

Finely chop 25 g (1 oz) of the olives and slice the remainder. Transfer the dough to a lightly floured surface and work in the chopped olives. Shape the dough into a ball, put into an oiled bowl, cover with a damp tea towel and leave to rise for at least 1 hour, or until doubled in size.

Tip out the dough on to a floured surface and knock back (see recipe 248). Divide it into 8 pieces and shape each one into a flat round. Put a spoonful of the remaining olives in the centre of each piece of dough, pull up and pinch the edges together to seal and shape into rolls.

Put the rolls seam side down on 2 oiled baking sheets, cover with a damp tea towel and leave to rise for 30–45 minutes until doubled in size. Drizzle the rolls with a little oil, sprinkle with some salt and bake in a preheated oven, 220°C (425°F), Gas Mark 7, for 20–25 minutes, until risen and golden. Cool on a wire rack and eat while still warm.

129 kcals (539 kj) ■ **low fat** ■ **low GI** ■ **high fibre**

351 kcals (1465 kj) ■ **low fat** ■ **source of antioxidants** ■ **source of vitamin E**

253 Wholemeal soda bread 254 Chive and onion bread

Preparation time:	250 g (8 oz) plain white flour	Preparation time:	500 g (1 lb) strong plain flour, plus extra
20 minutes	**1 teaspoon bicarbonate of soda**	**20 minutes, plus rising**	**for dusting**
	2 teaspoons cream of tartar		**7 g (¼ oz) sachet fast-action dried yeast**
Cooking time:	**2 teaspoons salt**	Cooking time:	**1 teaspoon salt**
25–30 minutes	**375 g (12 oz) plain wholemeal flour, plus**	**20–30 minutes**	**15 g (½ oz) low-fat spread**
	extra for dusting and sprinkling		**300–400 ml (½ pint–14 fl oz) warm water**
Oven temperature:	**300 ml (½ pint) semi-skimmed milk**	Oven temperature:	**1 bunch of chives, snipped**
220°C (425°F) Gas Mark 7	**4 tablespoons water**	**220°C (425°F) Gas Mark 7**	**1 onion, finely chopped**
			salt, for sprinkling

Serves: **8**

Serves: **8**

Sift the white flour, bicarbonate of soda, cream of tartar and salt into a large bowl. Stir in the wholemeal flour, then add the milk and measurement water and mix to a soft dough.

Turn out the dough on to a floured surface, knead lightly, then shape into a large round about 5 cm (2 inches) thick.

Put the loaf on a floured baking sheet, cut a deep cross in the top and sprinkle with flour. Bake in a preheated oven, 220°C (425°F), Gas Mark 7, for 25–30 minutes. Cool on a wire rack.

Sift the flour into a large bowl and add the yeast and salt. Add the low-fat spread the rub in with the fingertips. Make a well in the centre. Pour in the measurement water and bring the mixture together with a round-bladed knife.

Turn out the dough on to a floured surface and knead for 10 minutes, or until the dough is soft and elastic. Put the dough into a clean bowl and cover with a damp tea towel. Leave to rise in a warm place for 1 hour, or until it has doubled in size.

Tip out the dough on to a floured surface and knock back (see recipe 248). Knead for 5 minutes, then work in the chives and onion. Transfer the dough to a 23 x 15 cm (9 x 6 inch) nonstick roasting tin. Flatten the dough with your hands, then cover with a damp tea towel and leave to rise for 1 hour, or until doubled in size again.

When the dough has risen, make dents all over the surface with your finger or the end of a wooden spoon. Sprinkle with salt and bake in a preheated oven, 220°C (425°F), Gas Mark 7, for 20–30 minutes, or until the loaf is golden and sounds hollow when tapped on the base.

NUTRITIONAL INFORMATION Wholegrain, wholemeal and brown breads give us energy and contain B vitamins, vitamin E, fibre and a wide range of minerals.

276 kcals (1154 kj) ■ low fat ■ low GI ■ high fibre

229 kcals (955 kj) ■ low fat

Preparation time: 15 minutes	**1 large egg** **200 ml (7 fl oz) low-fat natural yogurt** **25 g (1 oz) butter, melted, plus extra for** **greasing**
Cooking time: 35–40 minutes	**125 g (4 oz) fine cornmeal** **50 g (2 oz) plain flour**
Oven temperature: 180°C (350°F) Gas Mark 4	**1 tablespoon baking powder** **1 teaspoon salt** **pinch of cayenne pepper**

Serves: **8**	**1 large red chilli, deseeded and**
	   finely chopped
	4 spring onions, finely sliced
	125 g (4 oz) fresh or canned sweetcorn
	   kernels, drained and rinsed if canned
	50 g (2 oz) Parmesan cheese, freshly
	   grated

Lightly grease and line the base of an 18 cm (7 inch) square cake tin with nonstick baking paper. Whisk the egg in a bowl until frothy, then stir in the yogurt and melted butter.

Stir in the cornmeal, flour, baking powder, salt and cayenne pepper. Add the chilli, spring onions, sweetcorn kernels and Parmesan and mix thoroughly.

Turn the mixture into the prepared tin and bake in a preheated oven, 180°C (350°F), Gas Mark 4, for 35–40 minutes, or until a skewer inserted into the centre comes out clean.

Allow the bread to cool in the tin for 10 minutes, then turn out on to a wire rack. When the bread is completely cold, cut it into squares.

275 kcals (1151 kj) ■ **low fat** ■ **source of protein**

Preparation time: 25 minutes, plus rising	**450 g (14½ oz) plain wholemeal flour, plus** **extra for dusting** **1 teaspoon salt**
Cooking time: 30–35 minutes	**100 g (3½ oz) mixed seeds (such as** **pumpkin, sunflower and poppy)** **25 g (1 oz) bulgar wheat**

Oven temperature:
220°C (425°F) Gas Mark 7
	1½ x 7 g (¼ oz) sachets fast-action dried
	   yeast
	50 g (2 oz) mixed nuts (such as hazelnuts
	   and walnuts), chopped

Serves: **8**	**6 spring onions, sliced** **50 g (2 oz) Parmesan cheese, freshly** **grated** **1 tablespoon clear honey** **300 ml (½ pint) warm water** **vegetable oil, for oiling**

Mix together all the ingredients, except the honey and measurement water, in a large bowl. Blend the honey with the water, then stir into the flour mixture and form into a dough.

Transfer the dough to a lightly floured surface and knead for about 5 minutes until smooth. Put it into a lightly oiled bowl, cover with a damp tea towel and leave to rise in a warm place for 2 hours, or until doubled in size.

Knead the dough, shape into a round and put on a baking sheet. Cover with a damp tea towel and leave to rise again for 1 hour. Bake in a preheated oven, 220°C (425°F), Gas Mark 7, for 30–35 minutes until the loaf sounds hollow when tapped on the base.

346 kcals (1445 kj) ■ **low GI** ■ **high fibre** ■ **source of phytoestrogens** ■ **source of vitamins B and E**

Index

Acknowledgements

Main photography by © Octopus Publishing Group Limited/William Reavell.

Other photography:
Octopus Publishing Group Limited 152 right/**Stephen Conroy** 26 right, 80 right, 88 left, 91 right, 94 right, 130 bottom left, 142 right, 143 left, 143 right/**Jeremy Hopley** 53 left, 71 left, 92 right/**David Jordan** 10 bottom right, 14 right, 46 top right, 56 left, 62 top left, 65 right, 66 left, 103 right, 146 top right, 150 left/**Graham Kirk** 135 left/**Sandra Lane** 27 right, 28 right, 50 right, 57 left, 113 left/**William Lingwood** 8 top left, 10 top left, 10 top right, 10 bottom left, 12 right, 13 right, 14 left, 15 left, 17 right, 18 left, 18 right, 20 bottom right, 27 left, 29 right, 38 right, 45 left, 58 left, 60 right, 64 left, 79 left, 79 right, 89 right, 99 right, 102 left, 108 left, 115 left, 115 right, 116 right, 118 right, 119 left, 121 right, 124 right, 130 top left, 133 right, 141 left, 144 left, 144 right, 146 top left, 148 right, 149 left, 157 left/**David Loftus** 32 bottom right, 35 right, 106 left/**Neil Mersh** 16 right, 23 left, 25 right, 32 top right, 37 right, 42 left, 42 right, 86 left, 105 left, 116 left, 120 right, 132 right, 133 left, 134 left, 134 right, 139 right/**Diana Miller** 31 right/**Hilary Moore** 68 left, 69 right, 96 bottom left, 109 left, 118 left/**Vernon Morgan** 137 left/**Peter Myers** 130 top right, 137 right/**Sean Myers** 28 left, 40 left, 40 right, 41 left, 41 right, 43 left, 46 bottom right, 54 left, 55 left, 55 right, 59 right, 60 left, 62 bottom right, 65 left, 69 left, 70 left, 71 right, 72 right, 73 left, 78 left, 83 right, 84 bottom right, 86 right, 90 left, 90 right, 91 left, 92 left, 95 right, 102 right, 103 left, 104 right, 106 right, 107 left, 107 right, 135 right, 136 left/**Ian O'Leary** 145 right/**Lis Parsons** 8 top right, 16 left, 19 right, 22 left, 30 right, 62 bottom left, 74 right, 81 right, 82 left, 129 right, 138 left/**Gareth Sambidge** 2, 17 left, 24 left, 25 left, 32 bottom left, 34 right, 36 left, 39 left, 43 right, 44 left, 44 right, 52 left, 53 right, 64 right, 68 right, 70 right, 73 right, 75 right, 77 left, 77 right, 81 left, 83 left, 95 left, 96 top right, 99 left, 101 right, 104 left, 123 left, 128 right, 148 left, 157 right/**Simon Smith** 6, 8 bottom left, 20 top right, 20 bottom left, 26 left, 29 left, 31 left, 34 left, 51 left, 51 right, 56 right, 62 top right, 74 left, 75 left, 76 right, 80 left, 82 right, 84 top left, 84 top right, 87 left, 87 right, 93 left, 93 right, 96 top left, 98 left, 98 right, 100 left, 101 left, 109 right, 110 bottom left, 114 right, 117 right, 119 right, 120 left, 122 left, 122 right, 126 right, 127 left, 130 bottom right, 132 left, 138 right, 146 bottom right, 146 bottom left, 151 left, 151 right, 153 left, 153 right, 154 left, 155 left, 156 right/**Ian Wallace** 46 bottom left, 57 right, 58 right, 142 left, 155 right/**Philip Webb** 32 top left, 37 left, 84 bottom left, 94 left, 96 bottom right, 100 right, 141 right.

Executive Editor Nicola Hill

Project Editor Leanne Bryan

Executive Art Editor Jo MacGregor

Designer Ginny Zeal

Production Controller Manjit Sihra

Picture Library Manager Jennifer Veall

Nutritional Analysts Carol Bateman, Kellie Collins and Barbara Wilson